on track ...
Eric Clapton
solo

every album, every song

Andrew Wild

sonicbondpublishing.com

on track ...
Eric Clapton
solo

every album, every song

Andrew Wild

sonicbondpublishing.com

Sonicbond Publishing Limited
www.sonicbondpublishing.co.uk
Email: info@sonicbondpublishing.co.uk

First Published in the United Kingdom 2021
First Published in the United States 2021

British Library Cataloguing in Publication Data:
A Catalogue record for this book is available from the British Library

Copyright Andrew Wild 2021

ISBN 978-1-78952-141-2

Typeset in ITC Garamond & ITC Avant Garde
Printed and bound in England

Graphic design and typesetting: Full Moon Media

For Albert, May, Arthur and Florrie

And to Amanda, Rosie and Amy, with love

Thank you, Jon Duttweiler
A grateful 'thank you' to Sam Smyth.

Unless otherwise stated, all direct quotes from Eric Clapton are taken from his autobiography *Clapton* published in 2007. All direct quotes from B.B. King are taken from a 2000 interview with *Rolling Stone*.

on track ...

Eric Clapton solo

Contents

Introduction

One of the 'Damascus moments' for me as a music fan was when I first saw Martin Scorcese's 1978 film *The Last Waltz*. This was, as I recall, in late 1982 or early 1983. I was sixteen. That film showcased the final concert of The Band, recorded in San Francisco in November 1976. The four-hour concert included guest appearances by the cream of the 1960s-1970s rock elite: Van Morrison, Eric Clapton, Neil Diamond, Dr John, Joni Mitchell, Ringo Starr, Ronnie Wood, Neil Young, The Band's former employers Ronnie Hawkins and Bob Dylan, as well as Paul Butterfield, Bobby Charles and Muddy Waters. Eric Clapton performed the old Bobby 'Blue' Bland fast blues 'Further On up the Road' and was so excited that he nearly dropped his guitar. *The Last Waltz* remains the greatest concert film of them all.

Around this time, my French teacher, I wish I could remember his name, gave me two C90 cassettes – live albums by Van Morrison (*It's Too Late To Stop Now*) and Eric Clapton (*Just One Night*). These two albums must still rank highly in the best live albums of all time.

I was now a fan of Eric Clapton's work and started collecting his large and varied back catalogue.

On 27 June 1984, my eighteenth birthday, I saw Clapton in concert at the NEC in Birmingham. His role as lead guitarist in Roger Waters' band was uneasy and fraught with tension. But his playing was astounding. A few weeks later, I saw Clapton as a surprise encore guest at Bob Dylan's Wembley Stadium concert – sharing a stage and a handful of songs with Dylan, Carlos Santana, Chrissie Hynde, Mick Taylor, Ian McLagan and Van Morrison. That was quite a night. Back at the NEC in March 1985, I finally saw an Eric Clapton solo concert promoting *Behind the Sun*. The following July, the astonishing four-piece Eric Clapton / Phil Collins / Greg Phillinganes / Nathan East line-up performed two hours of peerless 1980s blues/rock, filmed for TV's *The Tube*. In these days of live shows going on sale a year or more ahead of a tour, I remember buying tickets at Piccadilly Records four days ahead of the concert.

Nine months later, in Manchester, with Collins swapped for Steve Ferrone, that four-piece was extended to five, with a certain M. Knopfler of Gosforth, Tyne & Wear sprinkling six-string fairy dust over a peerless set of songs from the previous two decades.

Of course, as an inveterate collector, I have since accumulated every available note of Clapton's music, including dozens of bootlegs and (as far as I can tell) all of the guest sessions he's played on since 1963. This project has also unearthed some beautiful music which had passed me by, such as Françoise Hardy's 'Contre Vents et Marées' or Clapton's own 'Danny Boy'. Listening to the original blues songs that inspired *From the Cradle*, *Riding With the King*, and *Me and Mr Johnson* has been an education and a pleasure.

Eric Clapton's career is simply too long and varied for a single book. *Eric Clapton: The Solo Years* covers every song on every studio album and single since his 'comeback' in 1974, together with the many live albums, soundtracks and compilations. Later books will cover his work between 1963 and 1973 and his sessions for others.

Eric Clapton is now semi-retired, content to sit on his laurels. Quite right too. Meanwhile, let us re-evaluate his significant body of work since 1974 when *461 Ocean Boulevard* reached the top 3 in both the UK and the US.

Andrew Wild
Rainow, 2021

Eric Clapton Before 1974

'Eric Clapton is God', the walls of London read in the mid-1960s, if you believe the hype.

Certainly, by 1974 and the release of *461 Ocean Boulevard*, Eric Patrick Clapton–born in Ripley, Surrey, on 30 March 1945–had made his mark as a guitar player of rare skill and attack.

'It was just graffiti,' Clapton told *Rolling Stone* in 1988. 'It didn't have any deep meaning. It was just a kind of accolade. They could have said anything, 'Clapton is fantastic....' It was nice, and I didn't argue with it. I have never yet understood what the fuss was about.' Eric, interviewed by Alex Coletti in 2007:

The first guitar I ever had was a gut-string Spanish guitar, and I couldn't really get the hang of it. I was only thirteen, and I talked my grandparents into buying it for me. I tried and tried and tried but got nowhere with it. I finally gave up after a year and a half. I started getting interested in the guitar again after hearing Muddy Waters because it sounded like it was easier–wrong! I wanted an electric guitar and, again, I talked my grandparents into buying me one. And, actually, within a very short period of time, I got somewhere with it. I bumped into people who had the same interests–who liked Muddy Waters, Little Walter, Big Bill Broonzy, Robert Johnson. And those people were the original Yardbirds; we used to play together a lot at parties and ended up forming an official band.

He joined The Yardbirds in October 1963, aged eighteen, after short spells in local bands. The Yardbirds tried very hard to be authentic, even touring as the backing band for American blues wailer Sonny Boy Williamson, but had little commercial success initially.

Clapton riled against The Yardbirds' plan to release a pop single; he abruptly left the band on 25 March 1965, the day 'For Your Love' was released. 'Totally disillusioned,' Clapton wrote later, 'I was at that point ready to quit the music business altogether.'

The Yardbirds recruited Jeff Beck, then Jimmy Page, but despite the post-Clapton hit singles 'Heart Full of Soul', 'Shapes of Things' and 'Over Under Sideways Down', failed to find a strong identity. They would eventually mutate into Led Zeppelin.

But it was the B-side of 'For Your Love' that gave Clapton the direction he sought. 'Got To Hurry' is a ground-breaking, blues-based guitar instrumental. No one in the UK played guitar like this in 1965. Eric, to *Rolling Stone* in 1988:

You can count on one hand how many white guitar players were playing the blues at the time. I'm not going to say Keith Richards and Brian Jones weren't doing it, but they were more into Chuck Berry and Bo Diddley. I wanted to be more like Freddy King and B. B. King. So I had no competition.

As John Mayall said to *Guitar World* in 2020:

> I saw Eric very early on with The Yardbirds a couple of times. He was the
> only one in the band that was any use at all – to my ears anyway. Eric was
> the only one I'd heard in England who had any idea of what the blues was
> about. The others didn't have what Eric had – but then nobody [else] has
> what Eric had.

**By early 1965, John Mayall, already 32, was one of the most successful
musicians on the British blues circuit. He had a recording contract with Decca,
and a permanent professional band, The Bluesbreakers, which included future
Fleetwood Mac bassist John McVie. As Eric told *Classic Rock* in 2016:**

> John [Mayall] was a blues archivist. He had the best collection of blues forty-
> fives – Chicago blues, everything – I'd ever seen in my life. He was a scholar.
> When he offered me the job [in his band] he offered me a place to live too,
> in Lee Green. So I stayed with him almost the entire time that I was working
> with him. And during the day, I would just have all these records out on the
> floor, putting them on the turntable, learning, learning, learning. And that was
> all I did. I just studied. Because I realised right away that I was in the perfect
> environment. He only wanted to play blues. Sometimes it would get a bit jazzy.
> But he wasn't impressed by rock'n'roll; he didn't want to be famous; he just
> wanted to play clubs and have it be 'real'. And I thought, 'this is heaven'. I just
> listened and played and listened and played.

**Mayall and Clapton cut a couple of tracks for a single, 'I'm Your Witchdoctor'
and 'Telephone Blues', but in August, Clapton left for a jaunt to Greece with
a bunch of friends. Mayall soldiered on with a series of guitarists, including
Peter Green, who would permanently replace Clapton the following year.
Clapton returned in November 1965; the crucially important album *Blues
Breakers With Eric Clapton* was recorded the following spring. Remarkably,
this British take on American blues was very successful. The album was
Mayall's commercial breakthrough, rising to number six on the British
albums chart. Clapton's loud, aggressive, piercing guitar solos still have the
power to surprise the listener. Clapton himself, however, was getting restless
again. Eric, in his memoirs:**

> Though I was happy with The Bluesbreakers, I was also nurturing somewhere
> inside me thoughts of being a frontman, which had been evolving ever
> since I had first seen Buddy Guy playing at the Marquee. Even though he
> was accompanied by only a bass player and a drummer, he created a huge,
> powerful sound, and it blew me away. As I was watching, I was thinking, 'I can
> do that'. So when [drummer] Ginger Baker came to see me and talked about
> forming a new band, I knew exactly what I wanted to do.

The knowingly named Cream, with Clapton, Baker and bassist/vocalist Jack Bruce, combined both commercially successful hit singles such as 'I Feel Free', 'Sunshine of Your Love', 'Badge', and 'Strange Brew', with devastating musical dexterity. They were a major concert draw and one of the most important British bands of 1966-1968. Antagonism between Bruce and Baker created tensions in the band, however, and the expectation of having to play long improvised solos night after night both fuelled their fame and set the band up to self-destruct. The final straw was a review in *Rolling Stone* that called Clapton 'a master of all the blues clichés of the post-WWII blues guitarists' and later suggested that 'while he has a vast creative potential as a guitarist, he hasn't yet begun to fulfil it. He is a virtuoso at performing other people's ideas.'

Deeply disillusioned, Clapton jumped sideways into Blind Faith, a supergroup featuring the precocious Steve Winwood, still only twenty years old, and a rhythm section of Ginger Baker and ex-Family bassist Ric Grech. Eric in 2016:

> In its infancy, it was extremely good when we were rehearsing and recording, but once we hit the road, we all got just, like, rabbit-in-the-headlights syndrome. We just panicked. I panicked. We got the same thing [as Cream]: it was 'Supergroup II' – and I think that's the kiss of death. If you really want to kill a band, call it a supergroup and watch it disappear up its own arsehole.

Despite attracting over one hundred thousand people to their first gig, Blind Faith imploded after an American tour in July and August 1969. Their sole self-titled album was commercially very successful – it was a number one in both the US and the UK–and captured the band's unique mix of Cream's hard rock and Winwood's R&B/gospel vocals.

Not quite knowing what to do next, Clapton performed and recorded with John Lennon and the Plastic Ono Band in September 1969, then hooked up with Delaney and Bonnie Bramlett, who had supported Blind Faith on tour. The album *On Tour With Eric Clapton* was recorded in December 1969 and features fine playing from everyone involved. Clapton's first solo album was recorded during this period. It was produced by Delaney Bramlett with many of the Friends band, along with Leon Russell, Stephen Stills and The Crickets.

From April 1970, Clapton and the keyboard player Bobby Whitlock wrote several songs together and played a small tour of British clubs during August with the Friends' rhythm section. Preferring to maintain a low-key image, Clapton named this band Derek and the Dominos. The subsequent album, *Layla and Other Assorted Love Songs* remains his high point as a musician. A follow-up remained incomplete, as Clapton withdrew from public life following depression after the death of Jimi Hendrix, his infatuation with George Harrison's wife, and debilitating addiction to drugs and alcohol. A three-year career hiatus from spring 1971 to spring 1974 was interrupted by just three concert appearances.

Ultimately, Clapton restored his health by working for several weeks on the Shropshire farm of Frank Gore, the brother of a past girlfriend. Eric in his memoirs:

I took with me an acoustic guitar and some of my record collection, and since Frank turned out to be a huge music fan, that immediately gave us something in common. He was a great person to listen to music with and bounce ideas off of, and he became my sounding board as to how I was going to get back into playing. We were living in a tiny cottage with a couple of bedrooms, a kitchen, and a living room. It was pretty funky, but Frank was a great cook and we lived mostly in the kitchen.

With his drug habit kicked, and despite a complex private life that can only be described as chaotic, Clapton has enjoyed sustained success, both on record and on tour since 1974, starting with a top-notch album that would kick-start his solo career.

461 Ocean Boulevard (1974)

Personnel:
Eric Clapton: lead vocals, guitar, dobro
George Terry: guitar, backing vocals
Albhy Galuten: synthesizer, acoustic piano, ARP synthesizer, clavichord
Dick Sims: keyboards
Carl Radle: bass
Jamie Oldaker: drums, percussion
Yvonne Elliman: backing vocals
Al Jackson Jr.: drums on 'Give Me Strength'
Tom Bernfield: backing vocals on 'Let It Grow' and 'Mainline Florida'
Recorded April-May 1974 at Criteria Studios, Miami. Produced by Tom Dowd
Released July 1974
Highest chart positions: UK: 3, US: 1

By Spring 1974, Eric Clapton had overcome the debilitating drug habit that had kept him off the road and out of the public eye for nearly three years. He says:

I began to collect songs and ideas for a new album. I was listening to all kinds of different music and even trying to write the odd line or two. Needless to say, the blues featured high in my priorities, and I was getting quite excited about starting on something soon.

The link to this next phase of his career was a demo tape sent to him by Carl Radle, the Tulsa-born bassist in Derek and the Dominos. Radle had been working with fellow Oklahomans Jamie Oldaker (drums) and Dick Sims (keyboards). As Clapton wrote later:

Carl was a fascinating character. A Tulsa musician of German descent, he was quite European looking. He always wore pebble-shaped glasses in front of hair, balding at the front, and long and straggly in back. Though only three years older than me, he had an age to him and a great deal of experience and wisdom. He was a natural philosopher as well as a musicologist and had a wide taste in music from all over the world. We could talk for hours about anything from movies to hunting dogs, and he was a real soul mate for me. But of course, more than anything, he was a brilliant bass player, with a minimal and melodic style that really swung.

This loose-knit unit, called Tulsa County Band, would coalesce as the core of Eric Clapton's band for the next five years. The addition of session guitarist George Terry (a friend of a local keyboard player Albhy Galuten who also played on the sessions) and vocalist Yvonne Elliman completed the line-up.

For the sessions, Clapton returned to Criteria Studios in Miami–the recording location for *Layla and Other Assorted Love Songs* three and a half years previous. His manager Robert Stigwood had booked the studio, producer Tom Dowd, and flight tickets. Eric:

And that was it. It had all been prearranged, and they were just waiting for me.

The album is an accessible collection of bluesy songs, with a country and/or reggae feel, and more emphasis on songwriting craft than guitar histrionics. The lead single, a radio-friendly cover of Bob Marley's 'I Shot the Sheriff', would be a *Billboard* no. 1 and hit the top ten in the UK. The album is named for the address of the house that Clapton rented during the sessions, a fifteen-minute drive from Criteria.

Beginning with his excellent 1974 'comeback' LP, *461 Ocean Boulevard*, Eric Clapton began to grow increasingly confident and conscientious as a vocalist and song stylist. His blues were more traditionally rendered, with guitar riffs functioning as sharp, precise accompaniment. Tunes weren't merely frames for extended soloing. Clapton also began to acquire reggae, gospel, honky-tonk and country influences, treating them with all the humble respect he paid the blues. John Piccarella, *Rolling Stone*, 25 June 1981

'Motherless Children' (Traditional, arrangement by Clapton, Radle)

A propulsive, up-tempo funky shuffle with lots of overdubbed guitars and some lovely, fat slide guitar from Clapton. Clapton's new band are tight without being too slick; a perfect start to this second phase of Eric Clapton's career.

'Give Me Strength' (Clapton)

Released as a single, B-side of 'I Shot The Sheriff', July 1974.

Acoustic gospel blues, with Clapton playing delicate dobro and singing right from the heart. Utterly beautiful. Eric:

'Give Me Strength' was a song I had first heard in London during the early sixties. It seemed to perfectly fit the occasion and also gave me the unforgettable opportunity of playing with Al Jackson, drummer of the MG's and a legend among players.

A faster (and rougher) instrumental acoustic take can be heard on *Give Me Strength-The '74-'75 Recordings*.

'Willie and the Hand Jive' (Otis)

Released as a single October 1974. Highest chart placings: US: 26.

Slow, fun and sexy. *Rolling Stone*'s Ken Emerson complained that the song sounded 'disconcertingly mournful'. But we should praise Clapton's confident vocals here. Marc Roberty writes in *Eric Clapton–The Complete Guide to His Music* that:

> Eric's vocals had clearly matured, with fluctuations and intonations that were convincing rather than tentative as in the past.

The focus, then, on selections such as 'Willie and the Hand Jive' is on songs and singing, over flashy guitar solos and long instrumental sections. Clapton would stretch out in his concerts but based his early solo career very much on studio craft and his increasing strength as a singer.

'Get Ready' (Clapton, Elliman)

If 'Willie and the Hand Jive' is fun and sexy, then 'Get Ready' is just plain dirty. Clapton and co-writer Yvonne Elliman were in the middle of a passionate affair, evident in some of the charged lyrics. 'I've never needed a running 'round pissing hound / Checking out the bitches in heat,' she sings. 'You've got a lot of nerve, dishing out what you serve / Waggling your piece of meat.' What does she mean?

'I Shot the Sheriff' (Marley)

Released as a single July 1974, Highest chart placings: UK: 9, US: 1.

An inspired cover version, first recorded for *Burnin'* by Bob Marley's band The Wailers in 1973 and brought to the *461 Ocean Boulevard* sessions by George Terry. As Clapton recalled:

> It took me a while to get into it. I was coming from a completely different place. To break my inherent musical tightness down to this real loose thing was very, very difficult for me to assimilate. The only way I could stamp my personality onto it was to sing it and just play the occasional lick.

Clapton's arrangement smooths out the vocal melody, sweetens the harmonies and, remarkably, does not include a guitar solo at all. And yet this commercial and popular song was almost dropped from the album, as Clapton writes:

> When we got to the end of the sessions and started to collate the songs we had, I told them I didn't think 'Sheriff' should be included, as it didn't do the Wailers' version justice. But everyone said, 'No, no. Honestly, this is a hit.' And sure enough, when the album was released and the record company chose it as a single, to my utter astonishment, it went straight to number one. Though I didn't meet Bob Marley till much later, he did call me up when the single came out and seemed pretty happy with it. I tried to ask him what the song was all about but couldn't understand much of his reply. I was just relieved that he liked what we had done.

'I Shot the Sheriff' was originally recorded with a much longer outro; the full-length version lasts for almost seven minutes and can be heard on the soundtrack to *Life in 12 Bars* (2017). It was faded at 4:20 for the album release.

Clapton's success with 'I Shot the Sheriff' – it's his only number one single in America – did much to introduce Bob Marley to a wider audience. Clapton would usually remember to credit Marley whenever he played the song in concert. In a cruel irony, Bob Marley would die in hospital in Miami, about ten miles south of Criteria studios, seven years after Clapton recorded this song.

'I Can't Hold Out' (James)
Powerful, pulsing blues with another committed Clapton vocal and a sublime slide guitar solo.

'Please Be With Me' (Boyer)
A delicate and beautiful country ballad first recorded by the Floridan band Cowboy. The original featured Duane Allman on dobro, so Clapton may well have first heard this on the guitarist's posthumous *Anthology* album released in 1972. What's more, Clapton had been given one of Duane's dobros by his brother and bandmate Gregg, so it could be the same instrument featured here. Either way, it's a touching tribute to a lost friend, heartfelt, poignant and classy.

An alternative, faster, mostly acoustic take can be heard on *Give Me Strength-The '74-'75 Recordings*.

'Let It Grow' (Clapton)
'Let It Grow' is a beautifully produced, almost devotional ballad. It builds from a hushed whisper through some Beatlesque arpeggios to a stirring, swelling instrumental finale. It also has echoes of a rock classic from a few years before. Eric:

> I was very proud of my inventiveness in the verse [of] 'Let It Grow'. It was several years before I realised that I had totally ripped off 'Stairway to Heaven'.

'Steady Rollin' Man' (Johnson)
A simple, straightforward shuffling blues, written by Clapton's hero Robert Johnson, with rolling piano, a catchy riff, and some authoritative wah-wah guitar licks. Eric, to *Rolling Stone* in 1988:

> [He was] the real thing, and I was the imitator. That's fine as long as you keep it like that. But as soon as you start to do the real things yourself and try to compare it, you see how far behind you are. That is the difficult part. That

is what made me give up trying to be the 100 per cent bluesman. Because I realised I would always be that far behind my ideal.

'Mainline Florida' (Terry)
Released as a single, B-side of 'Willie and the Hand Jive', October 1974.

A powerful riff and tight arrangement push forward this excellent, upbeat rock song, which has a strong chorus and closes out the album on a high.

Other Contemporary Recordings
'Eyesight To The Blind' (Williamson)
A few weeks before flying to Miami to record *461 Ocean Boulevard*, Eric Clapton recorded two songs for the soundtrack to Ken Russell's film version of The Who's *Tommy*. Clapton:

> I had a call from Pete Townshend asking me if I would like to make a cameo appearance in *Tommy*, being filmed at Pinewood Studios. He wanted me to play an old Sonny Boy Williamson song, 'Eyesight to the Blind', and I was to do this in the character of a preacher in a church that worshipped Marilyn Monroe. I thought the whole idea sounded like a load of bollocks. They sent a car for me [and] I spent the whole time getting drunk with Keith Moon. Compared to him, I viewed myself as a lightweight.

'Eyesight to the Blind' uses the future Who rhythm section of John Entwistle and Kenney Jones. Clapton also performs on 'Sally Simpson', a country shuffle from side four of the original album. He's the only guitarist credited, with vocals by Roger Daltrey and Pete Townshend. Both songs date from March 1974 at The Who's Ramport Studios in Battersea, London.
  'Eyesight To The Blind' was added to Eric's live set in spring 1975 following the release of the film. A live version is available on *Crossroads 2: Live in the Seventies* (1996).

'Driftin'' (Moore, Brown, Williams)
A blues standard first recorded by Johnny Moore's Three Blazers in 1945. It was a feature of Eric Clapton's live set at this time; his version is closely based on Bobby 'Blue' Bland's 1966 recording. A 1974 live version is available on *EC Was Here* (1975), with two more on both *Crossroads 2: Live in the Seventies* (1996), *Give Me Strength-The '74-'75 Recordings* (2013) and, more recently, on *Slowhand at 70* (2016).

'Smile' (Chaplin, Parsons, Phillips)
The Charlie Chaplin song which opened live sets for a time. A recording from 20 July 1974 was released on the RSO sampler album *Prime Cuts* in May 1975, on *Time Pieces Voll.II* in 1983, and on *Give Me Strength-The '74-'75 Recordings* (2013).

'Little Queenie' (Berry)
Chuck Berry's 1959 single performed as an encore in 1974. A very ragged version can be heard on *Life in 12 Bars* (2017).

'All I Have To Do Is Dream' (Bryant)
The Everly Brothers' song played as a feedback-heavy coda to 'Badge' in 1974.

'Lonesome Road Blues' (Broonzy)
Clapton sings Big Bill Broonzy via Muddy Waters. It's a slow, acoustic run-through with an air of desperation in the vocal, but some sparkling guitar licks. On some reissues, including *Crossroads 2: Live in the Seventies*, this song is called 'Walkin' Down the Road' and credited to the otherwise unknown Alan Musgrave and Paul Levine.

'Ain't That Loving You' (Reed)
A half-hearted, slow Jimmy Reed blues with lots of slide guitar.

'Meet Me (Down at the Bottom)' (Dixon)
Hints of J. J. Cale colour this tasteful blues, which could easily have been added to *461 Ocean Boulevard* if edited from its over-long seven minutes. Also included on *Blues* (1999) and performed during the blues-only set at the Royal Albert Hall, February-March 1993.

'Eric After Hours Blues' (Clapton)
A slow, moody blues instrumental in search of lyrics. Also included on *Blues* (1999).

'B Minor Jam' (Clapton)
A loose seven-minute two guitars/bass jam, actually in F major. Also included on *Blues* (1999).

These last five named tracks were made available on *Give Me Strength-The '74-'75 Recordings,* released in 2013, along with two takes of a funky slide guitar jam called 'Getting Acquainted' and alternative takes of 'Please Be with Me' and 'Give Me Strength'. Other tracks from these sessions remain unreleased: 'Old Vibes', 'Something You Got', 'Eat the Cook', 'Gypsy', and a new version of 'It's Too Late'.

There's One in Every Crowd (1975)

Personnel:
Eric Clapton: vocals, guitars, dobro
George Terry: guitars, vocals
Carl Radle: guitar, bass
Dick Sims: Hammond organ, acoustic piano, Fender Rhodes
Albhy Galuten: synthesizers
Jamie Oldaker: drums, percussion
Yvonne Elliman: vocals
Marcy Levy: vocals
Recorded August-September 1974 at Dynamic Sound Studios, Jamaica; November 1974 at Criteria Studios, Miami. Produced by Tom Dowd.
Released March 1975.
Highest chart positions: UK: 14, US: 21

The quick-off-the-mark but messy follow-up to *461 Ocean Boulevard* was very much an attempt of 'more of the same'. But *There's One in Every Crowd* generally sounds tired and uninspired. Most of the tracks were laid down, with Tom Dowd producing Eric's regular band at Dynamic Studios in Jamaica in August and September 1974. Vocalist Marcy Levy was added to the line-up at this point. 'Opposites' dates from a later session back at Criteria in November. Eric:

> Because of the success of 'I Shot the Sheriff', Tom [Dowd] and Roger [Forrester, Clapton's manager] thought it would be good to head down to the Caribbean to follow up the reggae thing, and they arranged a trip to record in Jamaica, where they felt we might dig around and get some roots influence. We started it with the original idea of sunshine during the day and work during the night, and everyone just got lazy. It's the kind of record that if you didn't like it after maybe the third or fourth time, you wouldn't play it again, but if you did like it and you carried on listening to it, you'd hear things that were really fine, just little things in the background, little touches.

'We've Been Told (Jesus Coming Soon)' (traditional)
A low-key country-blues-gospel with more tasteful dobro and carefully arranged backing vocals.

'Swing Low, Sweet Chariot' (traditional)
Released as a single May 1975, Highest chart placings: UK: 19.

Perhaps not an obvious follow-up to 'I Shot the Sheriff', this reggae take on an old spiritual scraped into the UK top twenty when released as a single. It sounds professional but forced and has been ignored by compilers of most of the Clapton 'best of' albums. The earliest known recording dates from 1909 by Nashville-based The Fisk Jubilee Singers.

'Little Rachel' (Byfield)

A relaxed R&B song, written by Rockin' Jimmy Byfield who played the Tulsa club scene and recorded for Leon Russell's Shelter Records.

'Don't Blame Me' (Clapton, Terry)

A poorly executed sequel to 'I Shot the Sheriff', with none of the drive of the original. Clapton:

It felt like we were milking a formula ... and that almost always backfires.

'The Sky Is Crying' (James)

Written by Elmore James, author of many blues classics. This slow version is intimate and sensual and a highlight of side one of the album.

'Singin' the Blues' (McCreary)

Side two opens with an up-tempo, funky song written by Mary McCreary, soon to become Leon Russell's missus. It has one of Eric's few guitar solos on *There's One in Every Crowd*. A rocking nine-minute version recorded at Hampton Coliseum circulates on bootleg.

'Better Make It Through Today' (Clapton)

The album finishes with four Clapton originals. 'Better Make It Through Today' is the best song on the album. It has a warm, smoky, late-night feeling and a swirling organ/guitar solo section that lifts and swells.

'Pretty Blue Eyes' (Clapton)

Released as a single May 1975, B-side of 'Swing Low Sweet Chariot'.

A lightweight pop song which could have been written by Paul McCartney. The gut-stringed guitar suggests 'Tears in Heaven', twenty years in the future, and the vocal harmonies and arpeggios are very Beatlesque. Or sub-Wings, if you prefer.

'High' (Clapton)

'High' was first recorded during the sessions for Derek and the Dominos' second album and sounds very much like a stray track from *All Things Must Pass*, complete with George Harrison-style slide guitar and massed acoustics. George Terry tackles the bulk of the slide work, but we have some pure Clapton blues during the fadeout.

'Opposites' (Clapton)

The album finishes on a pleasant note with another Harrison-influenced track with an obvious Beatles feeling throughout, including some delightful vocal harmonies and delicate guitar interplay. Eric:

The last song on side two is 'Opposites', which Albhy Galuten and George Terry recorded on New Year's Eve. If you listen to the end, you'll hear them play 'Old Lang Syne.' I think it's Flash Terry's finest moment.

Other Contemporary Tracks
'Whatcha Gonna Do' (Tosh)
A solid reggae track recorded during the Jamaican sessions for *There's One in Every Crowd*. Writer Peter Tosh plays guitar and sings a verse. Tosh recorded his own version on Clapton favourite, *Legalize It* (1976). Available on the *Crossroads* box set (1988) and *Give Me Strength-The '74-'75 Recordings* (2013).

'I Found a Love' (Russell)
A focussed, rocking track inexplicably left off the final album. It would have made a great opener but remained unheard for fourteen years. Available on the *Crossroads* box set (1988) and *Give Me Strength-The '74-'75 Recordings* (2013).

'When Things Go Wrong (It Hurts Me Too)' (London)
A blues standard written by Mel London but most associated with Tampa Red and Elmore James. Years later, Clapton would re-record this for *From the Cradle*. Available on the *Crossroads* box set (1988) and *Give Me Strength-The '74-'75 Recordings* (2013).

'Burial' (Tosh, Livingstone)
'Burial' is a terrific reggae song recorded with Peter Tosh in Jamaica in August-September 1974. It would have perhaps been out of place on its parent album (or on any Eric Clapton album) but stands as one of Clapton's better experiments. Peter Tosh recorded his own version on *Legalize It* (1976). Available on *Give Me Strength-The '74-'75 Recordings* (2013).

'Fool Like Me' (Clement, Maddox)
Eric covers a track from Jerry Lee Lewis' Sun period as a blues shuffle. There's no reason why this was not included on *There's One in Every Crowd*, other than perhaps a surplus of songs. Available on *Give Me Strength-The '74-'75 Recordings* (2013).

'Teach Me To Be Your Woman' (Levy)
'Teach Me To Be Your Woman' is a powerhouse performance from the 1975 tour, featuring Marcy Levy singing her own song. It can be heard on bootleg. Another song, 'The Sun Is Shining on Me', is listed on some of the setlists of Japanese dates in October and November, but this may well be a misidentification of 'Teach Me To Be Your Woman'. No recordings have yet surfaced to confirm.

'Knocking on Heaven's Door' (Dylan)
Released as a single August 1975, Highest chart placings: UK: 38.

Eric Clapton worked with Jamaican-born singer and guitarist Arthur Louis in London in January 1975, recording six tracks. One of these was a soft reggae version of Bob Dylan's 'Knocking on Heaven's Door'. Six months later, back at Criteria, Clapton used the exact arrangement himself, recording it for a single with his regular band. It was a mid-chart hit for Clapton in the UK and is familiar from its inclusion on many 'best of' compilations.

'Someone Like You' (Louis)
Released as a single, August 1975, B-side of 'Knocking on Heaven's Door'.

A gentle, acoustic, regretful Arthur Louis song recorded mid-tour in New York in June 1975. This is one of those almost lost great songs that sit in every artist's back catalogue. Hear it on the *Crossroads* box set (1988) and *Give Me Strength-The '74-'75 Recordings* (2013).

No Reason To Cry (1976)

Personnel:
Eric Clapton: lead vocals, guitar, dobro
George Terry: guitar, backing vocals
Dick Sims: keyboards
Carl Radle: bass
Jamie Oldaker: drums, percussion
Yvonne Elliman: backing vocals
Marcy Levy: backing vocals
Sergio Pastora: percussion
Ronnie Wood: guitar
Bob Dylan: guitar, vocals
Georgie Fame: keyboards
Billy Preston: keyboards, vocals
Robbie Robertson: guitar
Rick Danko: bass, vocals
Garth Hudson: guitar
Richard Manuel: piano, vocals
Levon Helm: drums, vocals.
Recorded February-April 1976 at Shangri-la Studios, Malibu. 'Produced by Rob Fraboni in association with Eric Clapton and Carl Dean Radle.'
Released August 1976.
Highest chart positions: UK: 8, US: 15

By early 1976, the remarkable story of The Band was reaching the end of its first chapter. They had moved from Woodstock to Malibu in 1973 and opened their studio/clubhouse Shangri-La Studios in 1975. That year, they recorded *Northern Lights – Southern Cross*, their first album of all-new material since 1971's *Cahoots*. Eric Clapton recorded his next solo album at Shangri-La between February and March 1976, with his own band and contributions from all five members of The Band, as well as visiting friends such as Bob Dylan, Georgie Fame, Billy Preston, Pete Townshend and Van Morrison. Clapton recorded over thirty songs, with ten of these selected for *No Reason To Cry*, an intermittently strong album and a big lift after *There's One in Every Crowd*. Eric:

> This was a drunk and disorderly kind of album, and we didn't really know where we were going. Part of the problem was that the setting of the studios and the situation were so idyllic that I, for one, couldn't get myself together sufficiently to write any songs. Shangri-La was the finest studio of all to work in. It was all wood and the room you work in was originally a master bedroom or a playroom because [the building] was [once] a bordello.

We should note here Clapton's remarks at a concert in Birmingham on 5 August 1976, where he spoke out against increased levels of immigration to

the UK, saying there was a danger of the country becoming a 'black colony'.
It was an extraordinary outburst from a musician who owed so much to black
recording artists. He later admitted that his rambling, drunken and ill-advised
remarks that night 'were not appropriate'. In 2008 he told *Esquire*:

> One of the most beneficial things I've ever learned is how to keep my mouth
> shut.

'Beautiful Thing' (Danko, Manuel)
Written by The Band's Rick Danko and Richard Manuel, 'Beautiful Thing' was
the first song recorded for the album. It sounds like Clapton's Tulsa band
with Ron Wood on slide guitar. 'Beautiful Thing' is a laid-back but very tasteful
opener with strong backing vocals by Marcy Levy and Yvonne Elliman.

'Carnival' (Clapton)
Released as a single January 1977, did not chart in US or UK.

'Oi', Eric shouts, as this busy percussion laden, up-tempo Latin influenced
track sets a fine groove, taking the riff from 'Motherless Children' and
supercharging it with backing vocals and prominent organ. An earlier version
with The Rolling Stones, recorded at a drunken session in New York the
previous summer, officially remains in the can but can be heard on bootlegs.

'Sign Language' (Dylan)
A wry, charming duet with Bob Dylan on Dylan's own song, donated to
Clapton. Eric plays a tremendous dobro part, Robbie Robertson adds his
unmistakable lead guitar, and one can assume the rest of The Band are present
and correct here. Eric:

> Dylan dropped by and was just hanging out, living in a tent at the bottom of
> the garden. He would sneak into the studio to see what was going on. He
> would appear and have a drink and then disappear again just as quickly. I
> asked him if he would contribute something for the album, write, sing, play,
> anything. One day he came in and offered me a song called 'Sign Language'.
> He told me he had written the whole song down at one sitting, without even
> understanding what it was about. I loved the words and the melody, and the
> chord sequence was great. All in all, it's my favourite track on the album.

Dylan also offered 'Seven Days' to Clapton, who passed. Ron Wood recorded it
himself on his next solo album.

'County Jail Blues' (Fields)
Georgie Fame's piano, Eric's dobro and some tough electric slide (Ron Wood
again?) colour a blues lament, first released by American pianist Big Maceo

Merriweather in 1941. Merriweather's signature song 'Worried Life Blues' has been recorded by dozens of artists, including Eric Clapton. A more faithful rendition would be performed in 1993 during Eric's first set of all-blues concerts and released on the CD single of 'Motherless Child' in 1994.

'All Our Past Times' (Clapton, Danko)
Released as a single October 1976, B-side of 'Hello Old Friend'.

A delightful duet with The Band's Rick Danko. Danko's Band-mates Garth Hudson, Richard Manuel and Robbie Robertson are audible, too, and although the drumming doesn't sound like Levon Helm, one guesses that it must be. Clapton would sing this song with The Band later that year at their farewell concert.

'Hello Old Friend' (Clapton)
Released as a single October 1976, highest chart placings: US: 24.

A self-penned single; commercial, but perhaps too whimsical to be taken seriously. The opening verse is 'As I was strolling down the garden path, I saw a flower glowing in the dark / It looked so pretty and it was unique / I had to bend down just to have a peek'. But songs like these kept Clapton on the radio, so they have their place in the back catalogue.

'Double Trouble' (Rush)
A highlight of the album, this is a scintillating Otis Rush blues track. It has lots of biting lead guitar from Clapton and someone, possibly Billy Preston, adds an amazing piano part. Rush's version dates from 1958. John Mayall's Bluesbreakers with Peter Green recorded 'Double Trouble' as a single in 1967.

The definitive Clapton versions are from *Just One Night*, recorded in December 1979, and a bootleg from Chicago in July 1985, both of which are in another league altogether.

'Innocent Times' (Clapton, Levy)
A country-spiritual waltz, co-written and sung by Marcy Levy and ladled with exquisite dobro from co-composer Eric Clapton.

'Hungry' (Levy, Sims)
Released as a single October 1976, B-side of 'Carnival'

Written by Marcy Levy and organist Dick Sims, this sounds like a rewrite of 'Any Day' from Derek and the Dominos' *Layla and Other Assorted Love Songs*. Even the arrangement with prominent slide guitar, organ and drums harks back to autumn 1970.

'Black Summer Rain' (Clapton)
The album ends with a lost gem; a heartfelt and straightforward rock song with a wonderful lead vocal and exquisite lead guitar. Marc Roberty in *Eric Clapton– The Complete Guide to His Music (2005)*:

> Eric brings 'Layla' to Shangri-La.

Other Contemporary Tracks
'Last Night' (Jacobs)
Recorded live at Eric's 31st birthday party when the tapes were left rolling, Little Walter's 'Last Night' is fun but inessential. It's a duet with someone (any suggestions?), and the lead vocals are, erm, well-lubricated. It is included on the 1990 CD version of *No Reason To Cry*. This song would also be performed from time to time on Clapton's 1978 tour.

'Tenho Sede' (Dominguinhos)
This is a Gilberto Gil song ('I Am Thirsty') which was performed by Yvonne Elliman and Marcy Levy in Portuguese during the Shangri-La sessions.

'Could This Be Called a Song' (Clapton)
Given to Ringo Starr, who recorded it with a modified title in June 1976, with Eric on guitar.

'Seven Days' (Dylan)
'Seven Days' is a Bob Dylan song first recorded by Ron Wood and attempted at Shangri-La.

'Big River' (Cash)
Johnny Cash's 1958 classic, jammed at Shangri-La.

'Adios Mi Corazon' (Simon, Clark)
'The Water Is Wide' (traditional)
'Idiot Wind' (Dylan)
Three songs sung by Bob Dylan during the Shangri-La sessions and released on the bootleg album *From Paradise to Shangri-La*. 'Adios Mi Corazon' is a Spanish language version of 'Spanish Is the Loving Song', 'The Water Is Wide' is an English folk song, and 'Idiot Wind' is Dylan's own song. Dylan is on piano, and various other participants take part – Eric Clapton is not immediately obvious on any of these, but he might be involved.

'Stormy Monday' (Walker)
'Hard Times' (Charles)
'Who Do You Love?' (McDaniel)
Three R&B songs from the Shangri-La sessions. T-Bone Walker's 'Stormy

Monday' and Bo Diddley's 'Who Do You Love?' are sung by Van Morrison, Ray Charles' 'Hard Times' by Rick Danko. Eric may or may not have been involved.

'Steppin' Out' (unknown)

An acoustic duet which could be Jesse Ed Davis and Eric Clapton. There is some tasty dobro work which is very Claptonesque. The song's title is speculative – but it's not the Memphis Slim instrumental that Clapton performed with John Mayall and Cream.

'What Would I Do Without You?' (Charles)

A twenty-minute version of a Ray Charles song, sung here by Richard Manuel of The Band. The bluesy guitar does not sound like Clapton, but he might be in the mix.

'Daylight', 'Beauty Spot', 'Let It Down', 'Disco', I Can See Myself in Your Eyes', 'Blues Jam', 'Do Bye Ah', 'Billy Joe', 'Tuesday's Tune', 'Buried Alive', 'Sooner or Later', 'Golden Slipper', 'Fever', 'The Path', 'Tried To Make the Devil Mad, 'Won't Somebody Tell Me', 'Right Now', 'It's Eric's Birthday'

Songs from the Shangri-La 1976 are listed by Marc Roberty in his invaluable *Eric Clapton: The Complete Recording Sessions* and/or released on *From Paradise to Shangri-La*. 'Golden Slipper' is the name of a Charlie Rich song, 'Fever' was written by Little Willie John and made famous by Peggy Lee. 'Let It Down' might be the George Harrison track. None of these have been heard. The rest remain unknown or impossible to identify with certainty.

'One Night' (Bartholomew, King, Steinman)

The Elvis Presley song, Marcy Levy's solo spot on the 1976 tour. The Dallas show on 15 November was recorded for posterity and syndicated for radio broadcast across the world, including John Peel's Radio 1 show in the UK.

'You're Too Good To Die, You Should Be Buried Alive' (Clapton, Wood)

Eric to *Sounds* in 1976:

> Woody came to stay with us at this house we were renting. He was pushing me around trying to get me to write songs, but I couldn't because the situation was so idyllic. We finally wrote a couple of songs that we didn't use. One was called 'You're Too Good To Die, You Should Be Buried Alive'. Can you believe that?

Slowhand (1977)

Personnel:
Eric Clapton: lead vocals, guitar
George Terry: guitar
Dick Sims: keyboards
Carl Radle: bass
Jamie Oldaker: drums, percussion
Mel Collins: saxophone
Yvonne Elliman: vocals
Marcy Levy: vocals
Recorded May 1977 at Olympic Studios, London. Produced by Glyn Johns.
Released November 1977.
Highest chart positions: UK: 23, US: 2

Slowhand was the first of his own album projects to be wholly recorded in the UK since *Blind Faith* in 1969, at the highly regarded Olympic Studios in Barnes, London. The Rolling Stones recorded six albums at Olympic between 1966 and 1972, The Beatles and Led Zeppelin were occasional customers, as were The Small Faces (*Ogden's Nut Gone Flake*), The Who (*Who's Next*, *Quadrophenia*), Jimi Hendrix (*Are You Experienced?*, *Axis: Bold as Love*), Queen (*A Night at the Opera*), David Bowie (*Diamond Dogs*), The Eagles (*On the Border*), and many others. *Blind Faith* had been recorded there in 1969. Many of these had been recorded and/or produced by Glyn Johns, one of the busiest and best-regarded British record producers. Johns had recently worked with Clapton during sessions for the wonderful Pete Townshend/Ronnie Lane album *Rough Mix,* recorded at Olympic in February 1977. Johns in his wonderful autobiography *Sound Man* (2014):

We had just finished a song called 'April Fool'. Ronnie had done a wonderful vocal and all we had left to do was the solo. We all thought a dobro would be a great sound to complement what we had done, and Eric offered to play it. There are a few moments in my recording career that I treasure, and this is one of them. Up until that moment, I had paid very little attention to Eric as a musician, and therefore never really understood what all the fuss was about. I thought he was just another bloody white kid playing the blues. That was very clearly my loss. In a matter of a few minutes, I had been completely won over. This was a perfect example of what I have always thought since about Eric's playing; he never allows his brain to get in the way between his heart and his fingers. On the last day of recording he asked me if I would consider producing his next record. I said 'yes' immediately.

Johns helmed a consistent, focussed, and tight album. Three of the songs became ensuring classics – 'Cocaine', 'Lay Down Sally', and 'Wonderful Tonight'. *Slowhand* was a big hit in the US – lodged at number two for several weeks behind the immovable *Saturday Night Fever* – as were the two singles taken from it.

'Cocaine' (Cale)
Released as a single November 1977, B-side of 'Lay Down Sally'.

A cover of a J. J. Cale song, first released by Cale in 1976. Remarkably, Cale's version was a number one hit single in New Zealand in March 1977, a few weeks before Clapton recorded his own version. This follows Cale's blueprint very closely, adding a touch more muscle and a fluid guitar solo. Eric, speaking to *Stern* in 1998:

> That's an anti-drug song. The fans only listen to the refrain: 'She don't lie, she don't lie, cocaine.' But it says, 'If you wanna get down, down on the ground, cocaine.' It's sad how young people destroy themselves with drugs. I hate listening to my old records, which I did stoned or drunk.

Clapton told Dan Neer in 1987:

> It's no good to write a deliberate anti-drug song and hope that it will catch because the general thing is that people will be upset by that. It would disturb them to have someone else shoving something down their throat. So the best thing to do is offer something that seems ambiguous. If you study it or look at it with a little bit of thought ... from a distance ... or as it goes by ... it just sounds like a song about cocaine. But in actual fact, it is quite cleverly anti-cocaine.

Eric told *Rolling Stone* in 1988:

> For most of the Seventies, I was content to lay back and do what I had to do with the least amount of effort. I was very grateful to be alive. I didn't want to push it. I was also tired of gymnastic guitar playing. And not only was I tired of it in myself, it seemed the advent of Cream and Led Zeppelin had woken up a whole spectre of guitar players who just wanted to burn themselves into infinity. The more I heard about that, the more I wanted to back off. I started to identify with like-minded people like J. J. Cale. When I listened to J. J. Cale records, I was impressed by the subtlety, by what wasn't being played.

J. J. Cale in a 2006 interview with Associated Press:

> I'd probably be selling shoes today if it wasn't for Eric.

'Wonderful Tonight' (Clapton)
Released as a single March 1978. Highest chart placings: US: 16, UK: 81. Live version released as a single in 1991 from *24 Nights*. Highest chart placing: UK: 30.

'Wonderful Tonight', one of Eric Clapton's most enduring and popular love songs, was written on 7 September 1976. He was waiting for his partner Pattie Harrison to get ready to attend Paul and Linda McCartney's annual Buddy Holly party.

I wrote the words for this song one night at Hurtwood while I was waiting for Nell [Pattie] to get dressed to go out to dinner. We had a busy social life at that time, and Nell was invariably late getting ready. I was downstairs, waiting, playing the guitar to kill time. Eventually, I got fed up and went upstairs to the bedroom, where she was still deciding what to wear. I remember telling her, 'Look, you look wonderful, okay? Please don't change again. We must go, or we'll be late'. It was the classic domestic situation, I was ready and she wasn't. I went back downstairs to my guitar, and the words of the song just came out very quickly.

Patti Harrison in her memoirs (2008):

I couldn't decide what to wear. I was taking a very long time to do my makeup and hair, putting on one dress, then another and another, throwing them all into a pile on the floor. Poor Eric had been ready for hours and was waiting patiently. While he waited for me, he was in the sitting room, fiddling with his guitar. He went through phases in listening to music and at that time, he liked a country singer called Don Williams. We talked about how beautifully simple his lyrics were, each song telling a story about everyday happenings. Eric had been thinking of writing something similar and had already worked on some music for it. Suddenly, as I was flinging dresses on and off, inspiration struck. When I finally got downstairs and asked the inevitable question, 'Do I look all right?' he played me what he'd written.

The song was recorded on 2 May 1977 in a single three-hour session. Production is exquisite, especially Clapton's sincere lead vocals and restrained guitar breaks. Eric, to *Rolling Stone* (1988):

There was an album I had very early on by Chuck Berry, *One Dozen Berry's,* and there were a couple of songs in there that were ballads, which almost knocked me out more than the rock'n'roll stuff. Because they seemed to represent him more, when his guard was down. I think it's the same for a lot of musicians. When you see them relax and they pick up a guitar, the first thing that comes out is a really nice ballad, the softer side, because they're so fed up with putting on this big façade.

'Lay Down Sally' (Clapton, Terry, Levy)
Released as a single November 1977, highest chart placings: US: 3, UK: 39.

Very obviously influenced by J. J. Cale, 'Lay Down Sally' is a commercial, bluesy country shuffle, co-written with band members George Terry and Marcy Levy. It was a huge hit for Clapton in America, his third-highest singles chart placing of all (behind 'I Shot the Sheriff' and 'Tears In Heaven').

'Next Time You See Her' (Clapton)
Clapton's close-miked vocals provide a tribute to the influence of country singer Don Williams. 'Next Time You See Her' has acoustic strumming, jangling piano and a tight guitar solo. It's utterly professional in execution and quite delightful.

'We're All the Way' (Williams)
A more obvious tribute to Don Williams; a straight cover of a track Williams had written for veteran Oklahoman country singer Jean Shepard. Glyn Johns' production is lush – tremeloed guitars, bubbling vibraphone, and gorgeous backing vocals.

'The Core' (Clapton, Levy)
A driving riff kicks off this up-tempo nine-minute duet between Eric Clapton and Marcy Levy, which is the centre point and highlight of the album. Guest saxophonist Mel Collins adds a new sound to Clapton's musical palette, and Clapton himself plays well, with a barrage of notes that recall his playing from the mid-sixties. Edited down, this might have been a huge hit single.

'May You Never' (Martyn)
Whilst Clapton never gets near the slurred intimacy of John Martyn's dark 1973 original, this sprightly version fits neatly into the overall *Slowhand* sound, even if the arrangement dilutes the stark message of the lyrics. It sounds like Eric is playing chords on his dobro here. Producer Glyn Johns states in his memoirs:

> One of my favourites on the album is the John Martyn song 'May You Never'. I think it is the ease with which Eric sings it that I like so much and the simplicity of the melody.

'Mean Old Frisco' (Crudup)
An Arthur 'Big Boy' Crudup blues song first recorded (also at Olympic) for Derek and the Dominos' abandoned second album. The electric slide guitar is tracked by dobro and Eric growls the vocals. Superior blues from a master of the genre.

'Peaches and Diesel' (Clapton, Galuten)
Released as a single March 1978, B-side of 'Wonderful Tonight'.

'Peaches and Diesel' is a shimmering instrumental with some gentle lead guitar and a beautiful melody. It ends this superlative and almost flawless album on an uplifting high note.

Other Contemporary Tracks

A 2012 deluxe edition of *Slowhand* adds four session outtakes and a previously unreleased live concert recorded in April 1977 at London's Hammersmith Odeon.

'Looking at the Rain' (Lightfoot)

Perhaps Eric was unhappy with his vocal here, recorded very early in the *Slowhand* sessions; there's no other reason why this lovely arrangement of a Gordon Lightfoot song first released in 1972 was not released on Clapton's album.

'Alberta' (traditional)

Part of his live acoustic set in 1977, this shaky 12-string studio outtake of an old Leadbelly song would be much later recorded in this exact arrangement as part of Clapton's *Unplugged* album. The May 1977 version can also be heard on the *Blues* compilation or seen performed live on *The Old Grey Whistle Test*. Eric, quoted in *Guitar World* (2008):

> It's an old Snooks Eaglin song, which is something I heard when I was very young. Snooks Eaglin's *Street Singer* album was an important part of my record collection. He was a great, great player and singer who recorded on the streets of New Orleans. The variety of his repertoire was absolutely amazing, but that song 'Alberta' was accessible to me as a beginning guitar player because it consists of three chords and just straight strumming. It just lodged in my head as a very sentimental song and part of my early influences.

'Greyhound Bus' (Clapton)

A gentle Clapton original, cute but perhaps not strong enough for *Slowhand*.

'Stars, Strays and Ashtrays' (Clapton)

A simple but terrific mid-tempo country song, but without lyrics for the second verse and an incomplete arrangement – the song almost falls to pieces at one point. It was destined for outtake status.

'Drowning on Dry Land' (King)

An Albert King song from 1969, also performed by Buddy Guy. Clapton recorded a version during the *Slowhand* sessions, but so far, this is unreleased. 'Drowning on Dry Land' was performed by Guy when he guested with Eric Clapton and Steve Winwood in Chicago in 2009.

'Dumb Waiter' (unknown)
'Looking at the Rain' (unknown)
'Be Bop and Holla' (unknown)

Three songs from the *Slowhand* sessions which remain unheard and unreleased.

'Rodeo Man' (Williams)
'Going Down Slow' (Oden)
'Fool's Paradise' (LeGlaire, Linsley, Petty)
'You'll Never Walk Alone' (Rodgers, Hammerstein)

These songs were performed on the first leg of Clapton's 1978 tour; covers of Don Williams, Champion Jack Dupree, Buddy Holly (or perhaps Don McLean), and the musical *Carousel*. The last two named are sung by Marcy Levy.
Recorded for radio broadcast but never officially released.

Backless (1978)

Personnel:
Eric Clapton: guitar, lead vocals
George Terry: guitar
Dick Sims: keyboards
Carl Radle: bass, backing vocals
Jamie Oldaker: drums, percussion, backing vocals
Marcy Levy: backing vocals
Benny Gallagher and Graham Lyle: backing vocals on 'Golden Ring'.
Recorded May-September 1978 at Olympic Studios, Barnes. Produced by Glyn Johns.
Released November 1978.
Highest chart positions: UK: 18, US: 8

Clapton's final album with his Tulsa band once again recorded at Olympic with Glyn Johns, who again applies a warm, wide and tasteful production with plenty of guitar. Despite having fewer 'hits', *Backless* is entirely the equal of the more celebrated *Slowhand*. Guitarist George Terry would not take part in the subsequent tour, on which Eric was supported by Muddy Waters. Albert Lee would join Clapton in spring 1979 and, by September, the rest of the band had been replaced as well.

'Walk Out in the Rain' (Dylan, Springs)
One of two fabulous songs given to Clapton by Bob Dylan. Both were co-written with Dylan's then-girlfriend Helena Springs. The first of these, 'Walk Out in the Rain', has a lovely bounce and swagger. Clapton's lead vocal is strong and confident: over time, Clapton's poise and vigour as a vocalist had increased significantly. Your author isn't too proud to relate that when he first played this on vinyl circa 1983, he listened to this song at 45rpm, concluding that it was Marcy Levy on lead vocals, not a speeded up Mr. Clapton!

'Watch Out for Lucy' (Clapton)
Released as a single September 1978, B-side of 'Promises'.

A shuffle, enjoyable and fun with some rollicking country-rock guitar licks. There is an uncredited harmonica player on this track which might be Marcy Levy. Levy's chorus harmony vocals are subtly perfect.

'I'll Make Love to You Anytime' (Cale)
A J. J. Cale track at that time unreleased by its composer. The close-miked Clapton vocal and growling wah-wah guitar is a carbon copy of Cale's style. Very good it is, too.

'Roll It' (Clapton, Levy)
Starting life as a studio jam of 'Before You Accuse Me', 'Roll It' is simple and

effective. Marcy Levy's lead vocal sounds spontaneous, and the music is little more than a repeated riff. We get some scintillating slide guitar, though.

'Tell Me That You Love Me' (Clapton)
A wonderful Clapton original – one of those deep cuts that are often overlooked in such an extensive back catalogue. It's reminiscent of the more country side of the Allman Brothers Band – 'Rambling Man' comes to mind. The guitar fills are delightful.

'If I Don't Be There by Morning' (Dylan, Springs)
Released as a single March 1979, did not chart in US or UK.

The second Dylan/Springs original here, tougher and with more snap than 'Walk Out in the Rain'. It was a highlight of live sets for the next year or so, and the version on *Just One Night* is tremendous.

'Early in the Morning' (Traditional, arranged by Clapton)
The obligatory slow blues, dating from as early as 1929, by American blues pioneer Charles Shand. Clapton's arrangement is closest to the 1965 version by Junior Wells and Buddy Guy; in 1991, Clapton would record a version of this song with Guy for *Damn Right I've Got the Blues*. The CD version lasts for close to eight minutes, two-and-a-half minutes longer than the vinyl version. Again there is uncredited harmonica.

'Promises' (Feldman, Linn)
Released as a single September 1978, highest chart placings: US: 9, UK: 37

A commercial, middle-of-the-road pop song; a top ten hit in the UK. It was written by Richard Feldman, the first of three co-writes on Clapton albums for the Tulsa-born songwriter. The co-credit is to Roger Linn, inventor of the Linn drum, the first drum machine. It's pleasant enough, but some sharp lyrics are hidden within its easy-going melody: 'I've got a problem / Can you relate? / I've got a woman / Calling love hate / We made a vow / We'd always be friends / How could we know that promises end?'

'Golden Ring' (Clapton)
A gentle song about marriage with sincere lyrics and the chorus: 'And though the times have changed / We're rearranged / Will the ties that bind remain the same?' Eric would marry Pattie in Tucson, Arizona on 27 March 1979. Eric, to *Flix* in 1999:

'Golden Ring' is the strongest song on the album because I wrote it because I was fed up with the general sort of apathy of everyone involved, and I just thought, 'Well, I'll take a song in there and whether they like it or not, we'll do it, they'll learn it and record it, and we'll put it on the record and that's that!' And if you listen to it, there's virtually nothing to it. Songs like that are caused by situations, but situations of that extremity don't happen every day.

Backing vocals are by Benny Gallagher and Graham Lyle, who were successful as a duo during this period. Clapton's hero J. J. Cale recorded a cover of 'Golden Ring'.

'Tulsa Time' (Flowers)
Released as a single March 1979, B-side of 'If I Don't Be There by Morning'

Pounding piano and driving slide guitar colour this in-concert favourite, written by Don Williams' guitarist Danny Flowers. The song had appeared on Williams' 1978 album *Expressions*. Clapton gives the song a snappier arrangement with a rock feel. Flowers, interviewed by *The Songwriter* web series in 2008:

> 'Tulsa Time' just sort of fell out of the guitar. I wrote it in thirty minutes when I was stuck in a blizzard in Tulsa. We had absolutely nothing to do; we couldn't leave, couldn't go home. A couple of months later we were in Nashville, supporting Eric Clapton [28 February 1978], and after the show we went back to Eric's hotel room, and the three of us sat around playing guitar. Don says: 'Play that new song.' So I'm playing 'Tulsa Time', Don Williams is singing harmonies and Eric's playing slide on a dobro. And I'm thinking 'this is good'.

Other Contemporary Recordings
'Before You Accuse Me' (McDaniel)
Two takes of this Bo Diddley song from the *Backless* sessions were released on the 1999 compilation album *Blues*. One of these almost certainly gave us 'Roll It', which has the same riff, tempo and key. The other is a tentative run through. The song would be revisited in 1989.

'Sweet Lorraine', 'It's A Shame', 'Eric's Thing', 'Depend on Me', 'Dickie's Song', 'Give It Away', 'The Road Is Long'
These are seven songs from the *Backless* sessions that remain unreleased.

'Sad Sad Day' (Morganfield)
A Muddy Waters song performed in concert in 1978.

Another Ticket (1981)

Personnel:
Eric Clapton: guitar, vocals
Albert Lee: guitar, backing vocals
Chris Stainton: keyboards
Gary Brooker: keyboards, backing vocals
Dave Markee: bass
Henry Spinetti: drums, percussion.
Recorded July-August 1980 at Compass Point Studios, Nassau. Produced by Tom Dowd.
Released February 1981.
Highest chart positions: UK: 18, US: 7

The generally excellent *Another Ticket* had two false starts. Clapton returned to Olympic with Glyn Johns in December 1978 and recorded three original compositions with Welsh session drummer Henry Spinetti (lately of Joan Armatrading's band) and bassist Dave Markee. Two of these, 'To Make Somebody Happy' and 'Cryin'', are solid performances and would have formed the basis of a good album. By the end of 1979, Clapton was using Spinetti and Markee as the core of a new backing band. Eric:

> Owing to prior commitments, George Terry left the band, and I hired an English guitarist, Albert Lee. Albert was a great guitar player I had known since the John Mayall days. Over the years, we became good friends. A rift began to form between me and Albert and the rest of the guys. By the spring and early summer of 1979, this division had grown into marked bad feeling. By the time the tour ended in June, things had got to such a bad state that I knew there had to be a change ... with great trepidation, I instructed Roger to get rid of the band. He fired them all by telegram while I looked the other way.

In September 1979, Clapton recruited the rhythm section of Henry Spinetti and Dave Markee and former Joe Cocker pianist Chris Stainton. It was Clapton's first all-British band since Blind Faith. The scintillating live album *Just One Night* showcases this first-rate group of musicians. Former Procol Harum vocalist/keyboard-player Gary Brooker was added to the line-up in the early weeks of 1980. A full album with this new band, produced by Glyn Johns, was recorded at Surrey Sound, a small studio above a dairy in Leatherhead not far from Clapton's home, in March and April 1980. But *Turn Up Down* was rejected by RSO.

Four of the tracks from the spring sessions were re-recorded at Compass Point in Nassau that summer, with five new songs making up the balance of *Another Ticket*. These sessions reunited Clapton with Tom Dowd, producer of *Layla and Other Assorted Love Songs* and *461 Ocean Boulevard*. *Another Ticket* would be Clapton's last album for RSO. With minimal promotion, it crept in the UK top twenty, staying in the charts for just eight weeks. In the US, both the album and the lead single, 'I Can't Stand It', made the top ten.

Orchestral synthesizers and piano glissandos lend an ethereal quality to the thematic inertia of *Another Ticket*. This becalmed resignation, like the more energetic downers on side two, is possessed of an eerie apprehension of death that lends such a seemingly light-spirited record its somber undertone. As an artist often criticized for mellowing out, Eric Clapton has succeeded in making very popular music from an authentic and deeply tragic blues sensibility. He addresses both the heart and the charts in the same way: with a bullet.
John Piccarella, *Rolling Stone*, 25 June 1981

'Something Special' (Clapton)
A relaxed, stately opener, a direct continuation of the slower songs from *Slowhand* and *Backless*. Eric's new band settle in with Albert Lee's and Gary Brooker's welcome harmony vocals sharpening many of the songs on *Another Ticket*.

'Black Rose' (Seals, Setser)
Released as a single February 1981, B-side of 'I Can't Stand It'.

A mid-paced, country-tinged Troy Seals and Eddie Setser song first released by the George Hatcher Band in 1978. It sounds a great deal like The Band.

'Blow Wind Blow' (Waters)
A straight cover of a Muddy Waters blues from 1953 with bar-room piano and a decent vocal.

'Another Ticket' (Clapton)
Released as a single April 1981, highest chart placings: US: 78.

A ballad of singular beauty – not so far away from previous successes such as 'Let It Grow', 'Peaches and Diesel' and 'Wonderful Tonight'. It has a looping chord structure and a vocal that moves from a whisper to a confident, almost aggressive chorus:

Every time you think you've paid the price / Seems you've always got to pay it twice / Every time you think you're near the end / You turn around and find another ticket.

'I Can't Stand It' (Clapton)
Released as a single February 1981, highest chart placings: US: 10.

Powerful, commercial, brisk, ballsy, dynamic, and a top ten American single, 'I Can't Stand It' is a tough sequel to 'Lay Down Sally' and 'Promises'. 'I Can't

Stand It' was the first number one song on *Billboard*'s Top Tracks/Mainstream Rock chart, which debuted in March 1981.

'Hold Me Lord' (Clapton)

A welcome return for Clapton's dobro, which colours this rootsy, up-beat country-gospel song.

'Floating Bridge' (Estes)

Blues from Tennessee musician Sleepy John Estes, first recorded by him in 1937. Clapton's version has a tense arrangement that threatens to explode but doesn't quite get there, despite a fluid guitar solo.

'Catch Me if You Can' (Brooker, Clapton)

'Catch Me if You Can' is a very commercial take on the J. J. Cale tough-shuffle blueprint. Clapton's vocals show a new confidence here and the guitar duelling is terrific.

'Rita Mae' (Clapton)

Released as a single February 1981, B-side of 'Another Ticket'.

A straightforward, fast blues which harks back to 'Why Does Love Got To Be So Sad?' but without the desperation. It has a long guitar jam between Albert Lee and Clapton, who plays his Gibson ES-335 from Cream days. It's the only time anyone really cuts loose on this album.

Other Contemporary Recordings

Three tracks were recorded in late December 1978 with Glyn Johns at Olympic Sound. They are available on the 1996 box set *Crossroads 2: Live in the Seventies*; the first two are also on the 1999 compilation *Blues*.

'To Make Somebody Happy' (Clapton)

Clapton's familiar descending chords from 'Let It Grow' and 'Wonderful Tonight' underpin a delicate country-tinged ballad that sounds like it has been wrought from the depth of his soul. An uncredited vocalist adds a high harmony. There are strings, too. An almost-lost gem.

'Cryin'' (Clapton)

A straight-forward rolling acoustic blues, predicting *Unplugged* thirteen years in advance.

'Water on the Ground' (Clapton)

A very simple, sleepy folk-blues which is clearly a one-take performance. Graham Lyle plays acoustic guitar alongside Clapton's somnambulistic vocals.

In March-April 1980 Clapton and his new band had recorded twelve songs at Surrey Sound in Leatherhead, Surrey, for a new album called *Turn Up Down*. 'Rita Mae', 'Hold Me Lord', 'Something Special' and 'Catch Me if You Can' were re-recorded later in 1980 for *Another Ticket*. The rest of the songs slated for release have been circulating for many years, as listed here:

'Blues Instrumental #1' (assumed Clapton)
A short extract from a slow blues jam.

'There Ain't No Money' (Crowell)
Rodney Crowell wrote and originally recorded 'There Ain't No Money' on his 1980 album *But What Will the Neighbors Think?* Albert Lee played guitar on Crowell's album, so is assumed to be the source of Clapton's cover. It's a gentle folk/country/blues song with a tasty, short dobro solo and some sweet slide guitar. It's not so far from early Eagles.

'The Game's Up' (Clapton?)
Eric sings in his lowest register in this laid-back J. J. Cale-influenced song, which would have fitted nicely on any of his previous solo albums.

'Freedom' (Clapton?)
A lethargic song which never really gets going; no one's heart seems to be in this at all, despite some spirited backing vocals by Gary Brooker. There is a reworked reggae version of 'Freedom' with new lyrics by comedy writer Ian La Frenais on the soundtrack of the 1985 film *Water*. It's performed by Billy Connolly, Chris Tummings, and The Singing Rebel's Band: Eric Clapton, George Harrison, Ray Cooper, Jon Lord, Mike Moran, Chris Stainton and Ringo Starr, with backing singers Jenny Bogle and Anastasia Rodriguez. It's not the best use of the talent involved.

'Evangelina' (Axton)
A cover of a top-notch country song from Hoyt Axton's 1976 album *Fearless*, sung here by Albert Lee. It's totally wonderful, but unfortunately out of place on a solo album by Eric Clapton.

'Home Lovin'' (Brooker)
Written and sung by Gary Brooker. As with 'Evangelina', it's a terrific song with some vitriolic guitar-playing and a great Brooker vocal. But it has no place here. Clapton was fond enough to re-record 'Home Lovin'' as part of the *Another Ticket* sessions in Nassau, but again the song was dropped. Brooker would release the Nassau version on his next solo album, *Lead Me to the Water* (1982).

'I'd Love To Say I Love You' (Clapton)
A country shuffle, again taking its lead from *Desperado-On the Border* period Eagles. The combination of dobro and honky-tonk piano is irresistible.

'Thunder and Lightning' (Clapton?)

A continuation of the same blues instrumental that opens the album. This track is listed as 'Blues Instrumental #2' in some sources. The Phil Collins song with the same name recorded the same year is a totally different piece of music.

'Oh How I Miss My Baby's Love' (assumed Clapton)

Not scheduled for release on *Turn Up Down*, 'Oh How I Miss My Baby's Love' has some choice acoustic guitar and dobro but sounds unfinished. With more work this could have been a keeper.

'Say Hello to Billy Jean' (Brooker? Clapton?)

Dating from the Nassau sessions, this slow, mournful song sounds like Gary Brooker's writing style, and he certainly leads the song on piano, and possibly shares lead vocals. Either way, this is too close to the superior 'Another Ticket' to have been included on the finished album.

'Lead Me to the Water' (Brooker)

'Lead Me to the Water' and another version of 'Home Lovin'' were recorded in Nassau, but neither would make the final cut of *Another Ticket*. Brooker would release both of these recordings on his next solo album, *Lead Me to the Water* (1982).

'A Whiter Shade of Pale' (Brooker, Fisher, Reid) and 'Mineral Man' (Brooker)

Gary Brooker's solo spots in Eric's shows in 1981.

'Setting Me Up' (Knopfler) and 'Country Boy' (Lee, Colton, Smith)

Albert Lee's solo spots in Eric's shows from 1979 to 1981.

Money and Cigarettes (1983)

Personnel:
Eric Clapton: guitar, slide guitar, vocals
Ry Cooder: electric guitar, slide guitar
Albert Lee: acoustic guitar, electric guitar, keyboards, backing vocals
Chris Stainton: keyboards
Donald Dunn: bass
Roger Hawkins: drums
Chuck Kirkpatrick: backing vocals
Johnne Sambataro: backing vocals
Recorded September–November 1982 at Compass Point Studios, Nassau. Produced by Tom Dowd. Released February 1983.
Highest chart positions: UK: 13, US: 16

1981-1982 was a period of great change for Eric Clapton. On 13 March 1981, seven dates into an American tour, he collapsed after a gig in Madison, Wisconsin. Hospitalised, he was diagnosed with bleeding ulcers and was close to death. Clapton, interviewed by *The Washington Post* in 2016:

I don't know how I survived. There was one point there where they were flying me to hospital in St Paul [Minnesota] and I was dying, apparently – I had three ulcers and one of them was bleeding. I was drinking three bottles of brandy and taking handfuls of codeine and I was close to checking out. And I don't even remember.

He spent several months recovering. Early in 1982, he checked into the Hazelden alcohol treatment centre in Center City, Minnesota.

Clapton, in his memoirs:

In the lowest moments of my life, the only reason I didn't commit suicide was that I knew I wouldn't be able to drink anymore if I was dead. It was the only thing I thought was worth living for…

This would be Clapton's first step to sobriety – although it would be several years before he would be free from his alcohol dependency. Meanwhile, his contract with RSO expired and Clapton chose not to re-sign. The 'best of' album *Timepieces* would be released in March 1982. 'Layla' was re-released as a single at the same time and reached number four in the UK in a ten-week run. This was his highest-charting British single since 'For Your Love' in 1965.

Clapton completed a short US tour in June 1982, his only live dates of the year, then commenced the recording of his eighth solo album – the first for his new label, Warner Brothers – in September. *Money and Cigarettes* marks the point where Eric Clapton's playing started to return to the fire of the 1960s.

The inclusion of six self-penned songs indicates a return of focus from previous albums. Retaining Tom Dowd as producer, *Money and Cigarettes* was started with Clapton's then-current band: Albert Lee, Chris Stainton, Gary Brooker, Dave Markee and Henry Spinetti. Clapton:

> I couldn't get any kick out of them for some reason. The thrill was gone, and there was a feeling of paranoia in the studio because they sensed it too. I spoke to Tom Dowd and he said 'Just be brutal. Fire them all, send them all home. They'll understand. And then we'll bring in some people.'

Lee and Stainton were retained, and *Money and Cigarettes* was recorded with a top-notch rhythm section of bassist Donald 'Duck' Dunn from Booker T and the M.G.s and just about every single on the Stax record label, and drummer Roger Hawkins, who has played on dozens of hit singles and albums by the likes of Aretha Franklin, Wilson Pickett, Cat Stevens, Joe Cocker, Paul Simon, Bob Seger, Rod Stewart and Willie Nelson. Chuck Kirkpatrick and Johnne Sambataro were both at that time members of the Colorado country-rock band Firefall.

Eric had seen a Ry Cooder concert in London in May 1982, and four months later invited him to add his distinctive slide guitar to the sessions. Cooder pushes Clapton hard, much as Duane Allman did in Derek and the Dominos. Cooder would support Clapton on his six-week US tour, his first for two years.

> Just as 1974's *461 Ocean Boulevard* marked a confident return from the drug-aggravated funk that followed *Layla,* Eric Clapton's first album for Warner Bros. is an unexpected show of renewed strength after a debilitating illness and too many sleepy records. Like most of Clapton's recent solo records, *Money and Cigarettes* makes no claim to greatness. Still, the simple, unaffected blues power at work here is surprising and refreshing.

David Fricke, *Rolling Stone*, 3 March 1983

In September and October 1983, Clapton performed in a series of charitable rock concerts in support of Action into Research for Multiple Sclerosis (ARMS). The first took place at the Royal Albert Hall on 20 September 1983, with Jimmy Page, Jeff Beck, Steve Winwood, Andy Fairweather Low, Bill Wyman, Kenney Jones, Charlie Watts and Ray Cooper. Shows in Dallas, San Francisco, Inglewood and New York City followed later in the year, with Winwood replaced by Joe Cocker.

'Everybody Oughta Make a Change' (Estes)
A clever reworking of a country blues from 1938 with both Eric Clapton and Ry Cooder cutting loose on slide guitar, one in each stereo channel. Clapton's arrangement borrows heavily from a version on Taj Mahal's 1968 debut album, which included Ry Cooder as a side musician. This swampy take is less urgent than Taj Mahal, but equally brilliant. Clapton's singing is especially strong. *Rolling Stone*'s David Fricke, reviewing the album wrote:

The electricity quietly racing through Clapton's crusty baritone and the saucy cluck of his and Ry Cooder's duelling slide guitars in the album's opener, a frisky cover of the old Sleepy John Estes number 'Everybody Oughta Make a Change', may catch you napping.

'The Shape You're In' (Clapton)
Released as a single April 1983, highest chart placings: UK: 75.

An urgent shuffle with multi-layered guitars and an uplifting rise to the chorus. Try not to listen to the preachy lyric. Albert Lee adds backing vocals and brilliantly trades licks with Clapton in the solo sections.

'Ain't Going Down' (Clapton)
A blatant copy of 'All Along the Watchtower', specifically the Jimi Hendrix version, using the same chord progression but in a different key. The Duck Dunn/Roger Hawkins rhythm section earn their session fees here in an impressively tight performance, and the production with counter-melody on acoustic guitar is pristine.

'I've Got a Rock 'n' Roll Heart' (Seals, Setser, Diamond)
Released as a single January 1983, highest chart placings: US: 18, UK: 83.

The lead single released a few weeks ahead of the album. It was written by Troy Seals, Eddie Setser and Steve Diamond. Seals and Setser had written 'Black Rose' on *Another Ticket*. Described by Marc Roberty as 'lame', this judgement of 'I've Got a Rock 'n' Roll Heart' is harsh. It might not offer much new to Clapton's fans, but it's thoroughly professional in execution and reached the US top twenty. The song returned to Clapton's live set in 2010 after it was used in a telephone commercial.

'Man Overboard' (Clapton)
An interesting verse and more Clapton/Cooder slide guitars take us to a limp chorus. This song is an attempt at commerciality that doesn't quite work.

'Pretty Girl' (Clapton)
A romantic ballad revisiting the descending arpeggios of 'Wonderful Tonight' and 'Another Ticket', but better than both. The lift as the song moves into major chords of the chorus is sublime. The solo is played on dobro and is delectable. Give this one another listen.

'Man in Love' (Clapton)
Released as a single January 1983, B-side of 'I've Got a Rock 'n' Roll Heart'.

A dirty blues-shuffle smothered in slide guitar.

'Crosscut Saw' (Ford)
Released as a single April 1983, B-side of 'The Shape You're In'.

A tough, down home blues arrangement of a song first recorded in 1941 but made famous by Albert King in 1966.

'Slow Down Linda' (Clapton)
Released as a single May 1983, did not chart in UK or US

An up-tempo country-rocker which veers towards a Cockney knees-up. Clapton and Albert Lee performed this song on Chas and Dave's December 1982 TV special. Chas Hodges was old friends with both Albert Lee and Eric Clapton. Lee and Hodges were in the much-missed Heads, Hands and Feet from 1969 to 1973, and Chas and Dave were the 'turn' at Clapton's 1979 wedding.

'Crazy Country Hop' (Otis)
Released as a single April 1983, B-side of 'Slow Down Linda'

A fun number to end the album. It's a rock-and-roll shuffle written by Johnny Otis, author of 'Willie and the Hand Jive'. Not to be taken seriously.

Behind the Sun (1985)

Personnel on 'She's Waiting', 'Same Old Blues', 'Knock on Wood', 'It All Depends', 'Tangled in Love', 'Never Make You Cry', 'Just Like a Prisoner' and 'Behind the Sun':
Eric Clapton: guitar, lead vocals, backing vocals, guitar synthesizer on 'Never Make You Cry'
Peter Robinson: synthesizers
Chris Stainton: keyboards
Donald Dunn: bass
Phil Collins: drums, percussion, synthesizer, backing vocals
Jamie Oldaker: drums, backing vocals
Ray Cooper: percussion
Marcy Levy: backing vocals
Shaun Murphy: backing vocals.
Recorded March-April 1984 at Air Studios, Monserrat. 'Behind the Sun' recorded at The Old Croft, Shalford, Surrey. Produced by Phil Collins.
Personnel on 'See What Love Can Do', 'Something's Happening' and 'Forever Man':
Eric Clapton: guitar, lead vocals, backing vocals
Nathan East: bass, backing vocals
Ted Templeman: percussion
Jerry Lynn Williams: backing vocals
Steve Lukather: rhythm guitar on 'See What Love Can Do' and 'Forever Man'
Michael Omartian: synthesizers on 'See What Love Can Do' and 'Forever Man'
Lenny Castro: congas on 'See What Love Can Do' and 'Forever Man'
Jeff Porcaro: drums on 'See What Love Can Do' and 'Forever Man'
Lindsey Buckingham: rhythm guitar on 'Something's Happening'
James Newton Howard: synthesizers on 'Something's Happening'
Greg Phillinganes: synthesizers, backing vocals on 'Something's Happening'
John Robinson: drums on 'Something's Happening'
Recorded December 1984 at Lion Share Studios, Los Angeles. Produced by Lenny Waronker and Ted Templeman. Released March 1985.
Highest chart positions: UK: 8, US: 34

Nobody ever said it was easy being God. With each post-*Layla* effort, Eric Clapton's message became clearer: I'm only human; allow me to fail. After his well-publicized bouts with drugs, and a string of lacklustre records, Clapton sounded as if he had finally gained control of his life and his music on his last studio album, 1983's *Money and Cigarettes*. Unfortunately, since that record lacked a solid single and was terribly untrendy, it was not a major success. Perhaps that explains why and how Clapton was persuaded to participate in the slick but inconsistent *Behind the Sun,* instead of the great comeback he seemed so ready to record.
Deborah Frost, *Rolling Stone*, 11 April 1985.

Behind The Sun **celebrates the first serious collaboration between Eric Clapton and Phil Collins. These two musicians would work together extensively, in the**

studio and on the road, over the next several years.

Clapton and Collins had been pals since 1979 when Collins was working on John Martyn's *Grace and Danger* album. Martyn suggested a visit to Clapton, a near-neighbour of Collins'. As Collins relates, Martyn was 'looking for something to, ah, brighten up his day and thinks Eric can help'.

Collins asked Clapton to record guitar solos on two songs on his first solo album *Face Value*. They become drinking pals. A few years later, as Collins writes in his 2016 memoirs:

> It seems that legendary producer Tom Dowd had mentioned to him that he should get a bit of 'that Phil Collins thing' on his next album, not realizing that we were buddies. So Eric decided to cut out the middle man and come straight to me. Frankly I had no idea that he respected me that much and would trust me with his new album.

Sessions took place at George Martin's AIR Studios in Montserrat in March and April 1984. The finished album is highly commercial with a slick eighties sound and some vicious guitar playing on two of the album's outstanding songs, 'Same Old Blues' and 'Just Like a Prisoner'. Eric:

> My disillusionment with my marriage was touched on in some of the songs I had written for the new album, like 'She's Waiting', 'Just Like a Prisoner', and 'Same Old Blues', all very personal numbers about the relationship between Pattie and me.

Though both were married to other people at the time, Eric Clapton and studio manager Yvonne Kelly had an affair. Eric Clapton's first child, Ruth Kelly Clapton was born in January 1985.

Warner Brothers, however, rejected his new album, which must have stung Clapton so soon after RSO had refused *Turn Up Down*.

'They said [the new album] had no singles and no relevance to anything else that was out there, and I needed to wake up and get with what's going on,' Clapton later told the *Edinburgh News*. 'Instead of getting arrogant and outraged, I did the shrewd thing.'

Despite being the musician who walked away from the Yardbirds because they had recorded a pop song, Clapton agreed to record four new commercial songs, all written by a Texan musician signed to Warner Brothers: Jerry Lynn Williams. These date from December 1984, nine months after the main sessions for the album. Three were included on the final release, including the lead single, 'Forever Man'.

As Clapton told *Q* in 1987, when asked about this move to commerciality:

> I suddenly realised that the Peter Pan thing was over. Because just before that Van Morrison had been dropped – mightily dropped – and it rang throughout

the industry. I thought if they can drop him, they can drop me. There was my mortality staring me in the face.

Now, I never wanted hits; I never wanted to have to deal with that. But faced with the prospect that [*Behind the Sun*] would be a flop, that it would be hard to promote, and that it was self-indulgent, I agreed to re-record a third of it. So Warners sent me some Jerry Williams song, which I really loved, and off I went to Los Angeles. There, in the studio, I met Greg Phillinganes and Nathan East. They'd been hired to play on the songs by the president of Warner Brothers, Lenny Waronker. I thought they were great.

Several outtakes from the Monserrat and Los Angeles sessions have been released over the years on singles, box sets and soundtrack albums.

If you've not listened to *Behind the Sun* in recent years, try a playlist of the original Phil Collins-produced album tracks and B-sides and rediscover a fabulous album which will enlighten and surprise you.

'She's Waiting' (Clapton, Robinson)
Released as a single June 1985. Did not chart in UK or US.

Phil Collins' pounding production marks out the territory for *Behind the Sun* – an 80s sound full of parping synthesisers, chorus-laden guitar sounds, Collins' rolling drums, and plenty of reverb. 'She's Waiting' is powerful and commercial but failed to be a hit when released as the follow-up to 'Forever Man'.

Eric performed 'She's Waiting' as the opening song of his three-song set at Live Aid. It was his current single at the time, but even this global promotion did not result in a chart placing in the US or UK.

'She's Waiting' was used in an episode of *Miami Vice*, the fourteenth episode of the fifth season, premiered on 17 March 1989. Clapton's recording is followed by an instrumental reprise. This is not a lost Eric Clapton performance – it was recorded by Marty Castillo for the episode.

'See What Love Can Do' (Williams)
Almost drowned by Los Angeles sheen and sounding very different to the songs either side, 'See What Love Can Do' is a pleasant but faceless song – 'the world would be so happy if we'd all just get along', Eric toots. Only an exemplary guitar solo, short and fluid, lifts this above mere hackwork.

Bassist Nathan East makes his first appearance on an Eric Clapton song here. East has been a frequent member of Eric Clapton's band since 1985. He has worked with The Bee Gees, Steve Winwood, Peter Gabriel, Bryan Ferry, Daft Punk, Herbie Hancock, George Harrison, Michael Jackson, Elton John, Barry White, Stevie Wonder and many others.

This the first of at least eleven Jerry Lynn Williams songs recorded by Eric Clapton. Williams break as a songwriter came in 1980 when Delbert

McClinton's cover of 'Givin' It Up for Your Love' reached the US Top 40. Bonnie Raitt, who had released Williams' 'Talk to Me' in 1982, included 'Real Man' and 'I Will Not Be Denied' on 1989's *Nick of Time*, which won three Grammys. Williams contributed five songs to B. B. King's dismal *King of the Blues: 1989* and co-wrote 'Tick Tock' with Jimmie and Stevie Ray Vaughan for their *Family Style* set.

'Same Old Blues' (Clapton)

'Same Old Blues' borrows a title from different songs by J. J. Cale and Freddie King and showcases Eric Clapton's newly vicious guitar playing. The pounding drums and Yamaha synths place this firmly in the mid-80s, but neither are overdone. The dynamics are thrilling – the verse repeats a simple chord structure in III – IV – I rather than the more common I – IV – V, and the whole song lifts moving into the chorus as the rich backing vocals kick in. The guitar playing soars above everything: stinging, powerful, fluid. Here is one of the great blues guitarists cutting loose. Over eight minutes long here, in concert, 'Same Old Blues' would transform into a twenty-minute showcase with multiple solos. All told a career highlight.

'Knock on Wood' (Floyd, Cropper)

A straightforward cover of the Eddie Floyd hit, written by Floyd with guitar legend Steve Cropper. Buddy Guy also performed this song, which might also have influenced Eric Clapton's version. It's a solid take, with Phil Collins' harmony vocals very audible in the chorus and hardly any guitar. 'Knock on Wood' was sometimes performed as an encore on the 1985 tour.

'Something's Happening' (Williams)

Eric's singing and playing are strong here on this reggae-tinged soft rock song, despite almost being buried by a very busy production. 'Ted Templeman's Doobie-proven cosmetic approach to production–the heap of synthesizers, conked-out congas, gooey cooing and tired Totos–almost buries the artist himself,' noted Deborah Frost in a contemporary review.

'Something's Happening' is notable for the first contribution to an Eric Clapton song by keyboard ace Greg Phillinganes who has worked on over one hundred and twenty albums by the likes of Aretha Franklin, Barbra Streisand, Bryan Ferry, David Gilmour, Dionne Warwick, Donna Summer, George Benson, Joan Armatrading, Leonard Cohen, Lionel Richie, Neil Diamond, Paul Simon, Roberta Flack, Stevie Nicks, and many others. He was a full-time member of Stevie Wonder's band from 1976 to 1981, of Michael Jackson's band from 1980 to 1991 and of Toto from 2005 to 2008. The rest of the band are no slouches: Nathan East on bass, Fleetwood Mac's Lindsey Buckingham on guitar and backing vocals, James Newton Howard on synthesizers (nominated for eight Academy awards for his film soundtracks), and John Robinson, one of the most recorded session drummers in history.

'Forever Man' (Williams)
Released as a single March 1985, highest chart placings: US: 26, UK: 51.

Hard-hitting, catchy and powerful, 'Forever Man' staked the territory for Clapton's sound over the next few years, forcibly shoving him into the 80s. It was recorded with the cream of the LA session scene, including bass player Nathan East, percussionist Lenny Castro, keyboardist and producer Michael Omartian, and both Jeff Porcaro and Steve Lukather of Toto. Lukather said to *Ultimate Classic Rock* in 2020:

> I talked my way onto that album ... I knew the producer on that one and I really wanted to meet Eric because I was a lifelong fan. I was so nervous when I met Eric – I have never been that nervous meeting any star in the world. I played for free on that album because I just wanted to meet him. We played 'Forever Man' and I froze up and I didn't know what to play, and that never happens to me. I would play a little bit, but I didn't want to play too much.

Clapton recorded his first music video for 'Forever Man', directed by Kevin Godley and Lol Ccreme, saying to *Ultimate Classic Rock* in 2020:

> It was fun, but it goes against the grain for me. It's a concession to the star-making machinery.

Maybe so, but 'Forever Man' was a US Rock Charts number one and provided the commercial success that the critical plaudits of *Edge of Darkness* and *The Pros and Cons of Hitch Hiking* had promised. It certainly helped that the opening line 'How many times must I tell you baby?' was a close cousin to 'What'll you do when you get lonely?' from 'Layla'.

In 2000, the Danish producer Michael Linde sampled and remixed 'Forever Man' into a dance style. Released as 'Forever Man (How Many Times?)' and credited to Beatchuggers featuring Eric Clapton, it reached number 26 in the UK charts.

'It All Depends' (Clapton)
A beautiful and very sad love song that has a restrained production, a rich vocal delivery from Clapton and a delicately-picked guitar solo.

'Tangled in Love' (Levy, Feldman)
Released as a single November 1987, B-side of 'Holy Mother'.

Spiralling synthesisers underpin another commercial song which belies Warner Brothers' insistence that there were no singles on the first, rejected version of *Behind the Sun*. 'Tangled in Love' is a classy up-tempo pop-rock song, co-written by old hand Marcy Levy, back in Eric's band after a six-year absence, and Richard Feldman, who had previously provided 'Promises' for *Backless*. Another Levy/Feldman song, 'Walk Away', would be included on 1986's *August*.

'Never Make You Cry' (Clapton, Collins)

A haunting ballad which features Eric, unusually, playing a guitar synthesiser – he is credited with this instrument on *The Pros and Cons of Hitch Hiking*, but it's much more identifiable here. 'Never Make You Cry' sounds like a eulogy for his marriage to Pattie by then in one of its troubled periods. Clapton's singing is a revelation, and he is subtly backed up by Phil Collins in the chorus. The lyrics are unashamedly romantic: 'I'll watch you fall asleep at night, I'll smile and kiss you, hold you tight / I'll hold your hand and close my eyes, it's here I'm staying all of my life.'

Gorgeous.

'Just Like a Prisoner' (Clapton)

A fiery guitar showcase with a real desperation in Clapton's playing and singing, probably his best-recorded performance of the 1980s. Some of the thumping drums and smooth synths sound a little dated today, but turn this up loud and revel in some of the most ferocious guitar-playing of Clapton's career – here is the power and fury of *Edge of Darkness* within a more traditional song format.

'Behind the Sun' (Clapton)

The delicate title track was the last song recorded for the album, as Phil Collins recalls in his entertaining memoirs published in 2016:

> Eric rings me one day: 'I've written a song that has to be on the record.' He comes round to Old Croft [Collins' house] with his guitar and sings it to me. I'm floored. It's fantastic and clearly deeply personal and pained. I say, 'How are we going to record this? The sessions are over; the album's done, everyone's gone home.' Eric says, 'We'll do it now.' He plays it once or twice, no more, and I record it. The meters are moving; that's good. Then I have to record his vocal. Again, I see the meters moving; that's a relief. Now we have to mix it. It's only him and the guitar, but for mood I put a little synth on it, nothing more than sustained strings. Old Croft is definitely not a good mixing studio, but Eric likes what he hears.

'Behind the Sun' is short, sad, and utterly beautiful. It's a heartfelt coda to a generally strong album. The performance is so immediate that there is a rare Clapton guitar error at 1:34. The outstanding vocal makes up for that in spades. Eric:

> This song expressed all my feelings of sadness over our breakup. I took the title from a line in 'Louisiana Blues', one of my favourite Muddy Waters songs.

I'm goin' down in Louisiana
Honey, behind the sun
Well, you know I just found out
My trouble just begun

Other Contemporary Songs
'Heaven Is One Step Away' (Clapton)
Released on the *Back to the Future* movie soundtrack and later on the *Crossroads* box set, 'Heaven Is One Step Away' is a limp reggae that plays for about ten seconds on the tramp's radio when Marty returns to 1985. Eric is playing the guitar synthesiser here.

'Too Bad' (Clapton)
Released as the B-side of 'Forever Man' in March 1985 and on the *Crossroads* box set. This is a tough acoustic blues, quite unlike anything else on *Behind the Sun*, which is perhaps why is was dropped. Here is Clapton doing what he does best.

'Jailbait' (Clapton)
Released as the B-side of 'She's Waiting', June 1985. It's an up-tempo, drum-heavy outtake that cops the riff from 'Layla'. It's a step below most of the other songs recorded with Phil Collins, so it's hardly surprising that it was removed from the album when more commercial material became available. This is only available on 7" single and has never been re-released digitally.

'You Don't Know Like I Know' (Hayes, Porter)
Released only in Australia as a single in November 1984, credited to Eric Clapton and Phil Collins. This is a superb cover of the classic Sam and Dave song from 1966, which has only ever been released on 7" single. There's no guitar whatsoever, but Clapton and Collins sing well together, and it's a shame that this hasn't been more widely distributed. The B-side was 'Knock on Wood'.

'One Jump Ahead of the Storm' (Clapton)
A song from the Montserrat sessions which remains unissued.

'Loving Your Lovin'' (Williams)
A two-chord Jerry Lynn Williams song with a by-the-numbers guitar solo. Released on the *Wayne's World* film soundtrack.

'Someone Else Is Steppin In' (LaSalle)
A stomping blues song, written by Denise LaSalle and first released by ZZ Hill in 1982. It was tailor made for being belted out by Shaun Murphy in Eric Clapton's 1985 live set. Listed as 'Steppin' Out' in every source book and online, this is the correct title.

'When Something Is Wrong With My Baby' (Hayes, Porter)

A classic soul ballad, written by Isaac Hayes and David Porter, first released in 1967 by Sam and Dave. It would be performed live in 1985 as Marcy Levy's solo spot in Eric Clapton's set.

Edge of Darkness (1985)

The producers of the tense political thriller TV series, *Edge of Darkness*, first broadcast by the BBC in late 1985, perhaps took something of a risk asking Eric Clapton to provide the score. Clapton's experience of writing to order was zero, so he asked American composer Michael Kamen to help him. They had previously worked together as members of Roger Waters' solo band on his *Pros and Cons of Hitch Hiking* tour in mid-1984. Kamen recalled, as quoted in *Spare Bricks* (2006):

> Eric got a call from the BBC to do music for *Edge of Darkness* and he was eager to do it, but needed some help. He didn't know the mechanics of film writing or what to do, realised it was just a guitar-playing score and asked me if I'd be interested. Of course, I said I was, because he's my hero – and now my friend – but my hero above everything else.

Clapton's playing on the six short tracks is incendiary: tight, taut, full of light and shade. It's absolutely right for the tone of the TV show. The soundtrack won the Ivor Novello Award for songwriting and composing and the 1986 BAFTA Award for Best Music. Kamen subsequently became one of Hollywood's most successful film composers. Clapton and Kamen would work together again on the soundtrack albums for the four films in the *Lethal Weapon* series (1987-1998), as well as the remarkable 'Concerto for Electric Guitar and Orchestra' performed at Clapton's Albert Hall gigs in 1990 and 1991. The tracks on *Edge of Darkness* are 'Edge of Darkness', 'Shoot Out', 'Obituary', 'Escape from Northmoor', 'Oxford Circus' and 'Northmoor', all written by Clapton and Kamen.

The year before, Clapton had helped Roger Waters with the theme music for the Stephen Frears road crime film *The Hit*. This was recorded at Rock City Studios in Shepperton in January 1984 but has not been officially released. Twelve years later, Clapton would provide the opening and closing themes to Frears' 1996 comedy *The Van*.

August (1986)

Personnel on 'It's in the Way That You Use It:
Eric Clapton: guitar, lead vocals
Gary Brooker: keyboards, backing vocals
Richard Cottle: synthesizer
Laurence Cottle: bass
Henry Spinetti: drums
Recorded September 1986 at Surrey Sound Studios, Leatherhead. Produced by Eric Clapton and Tom Dowd.
Personnel on all other songs:
Eric Clapton: vocals, guitar
Greg Phillinganes: keyboards, backing vocals
Nathan East: bass
Phil Collins: drums, backing vocals
Michael Brecker: saxophone
Dave Bargeron: trombone
Randy Brecker: trumpet
Jon Faddis: trumpet
Katie Kissoon, Magic Moreno and Tessa Niles: backing vocals
Richard Feldman: additional keyboards on 'Walk Away'
Tina Turner: lead vocals on 'Tearing Us Apart', backing vocals on 'Hold On'.
Recorded April-May 1986 at Sunset Sound Studios, Los Angeles. Horns overdubbed in New York. Produced by Phil Collins. Released November 1986.
Highest chart positions: UK: 3, US: 37

When you're in your mid-20s, you've got something that you lose. If I was a sportsman, I would have retired by now. You've just got a certain amount of dynamism that you lose when you turn 30. You have to accept that, otherwise, you're chasing a dream.
Eric Clapton, as quoted in *Q*, January 1987.

August was written and recorded in a period of significant personal turmoil for Eric Clapton. The album, originally titled *One More Car, One More Rider*, commemorates the month of the birth of Clapton's son Conor in August 1986. Clapton had a three-year relationship with Italian actress, model, and television celebrity Lory Del Santo. As Del Santo told the *Sunday Mirror* in 2000:

I got a call from Eric. He had tried to commit suicide by hanging himself from a tree. He had fainted, then realised he was still alive. I was in shock. Then afterwards I felt really angry and sad because I thought, how could he try and do this when we had a family to look forward to. I was angry that myself and the baby weren't important enough to him. When you risk dying at any time, life is too precious to waste like that. He found me a mews house in Chelsea and came to visit every day.

57

This episode finally ended Clapton's marriage. He and Pattie officially divorced in 1988. Songs written in this period, such as 'Tearing Us Apart', 'Take a Chance' and 'Holy Mother' reflect different aspects of Clapton's complicated life. Eric Clapton's tenth solo album is unlike any other album in his back catalogue. With Phil Collins producing once again, and with the high-class talents of Greg Phillinganes and Nathan East on display, *August* is a professionally recorded and very commercial album, which consists, mostly, of lightweight soul/pop songs, polished with a production sheen that relegates Clapton's singing and playing to the back of the mix. It is only on the mercurial 'Holy Mother' – the best song here by a long way – and on grittier songs such as 'Hung Up on Your Love', 'Miss You', and the B-side 'Wanna Make Love to You' that the real Clapton emerges. Eric to *Rolling Stone* (1988):

> At the end of the day, people will say that *Behind the Sun* and *August* are really Phil Collins records. Fine; if that's all they can hear, they're not listening properly. I'm in there with as much as I got, but not in a competitive way. If I did, it would be a mess. It works pretty good for me to allow people to be themselves rather than trying to lay down the law.

August was a top three album in the UK, where it certified Platinum sales in a forty-six-week chart run.

'It's in the Way That You Use It' (Clapton, Robertson)
Released as a single March 1987, highest chart placing: UK: 77.

Recorded six months after the rest of *August* and added to the album at the last minute, 'It's in the Way That You Use It' is a co-write between Eric Clapton and The Band's Robbie Robertson for the soundtrack of the Paul Newman-Tom Cruise vehicle *The Color of Money*. It's a powerful song, with a strong vocal, a bubbling bass, and positive guitar playing, despite the rare use of a trucker's modulation. Eric's band here includes his old friends Gary Brooker and Henry Spinetti, along with Welsh brothers Richard and Lawrence Cottle, both of The Alan Parsons Project.

'Run' (Dozier)
Written by Lamont Dozier, one-third of the Holland–Dozier–Holland team that wrote, arranged, and produced many songs that helped define the Motown sound in the 1960s. They wrote ten number one hits for the Supremes in 1964-1967, including 'You Can't Hurry Love', covered by Phil Collins in 1982. 'Run' epitomizes Clapton's new sound; tight performances, clean production, synthesisers and drum machines. As with much of *August*, 'Run' is commercial and professional but a little lifeless. Contemporary live performances of 'Run' were terrific and would be driven by Nathan East's pulsing bass.

'Tearing Us Apart' (Clapton, Phillinganes)
Released as a single June 1987, highest chart placing: UK: 56.

One of the songs I wrote while living [in London] was called 'Tearing Us Apart', which was about 'the Committee', the group of Pattie's friends whom I now blamed for coming between us.

'Tearing Us Apart' is a feisty duet between Eric and newly successful Tina Turner. Her up-beat approach fits well into Eric's new musical style; the band cook-up some impressive syncopations, and Eric cuts loose on slide guitar.

'Bad Influence' (Cray, Vannice)
Released as a single March 1987, B-side of 'It's in the Way That You Use It'

In 1986, Robert Cray was just three albums into his career, so a cover by Eric Clapton was a big career boost. Clapton became aware of Cray in 1983 when Duck Dunn played him a cassette of *Bad Influence*.
    Cray would work with Clapton on *Journeyman* and *24 Nights,* and also supported Clapton on tour on many occasions.

The hardest thing for me to come to terms with was that Robert Cray was an intelligent young black man who wasn't interested in making contemporary black music. He was more interested in preserving the blues form and enlarging on it. Once I accepted that, it was pretty easy for me to accept the rest. And it was fantastic to find out that he did know about my work and liked it as well as Hendrix and the Kings. The sides to that guy are phenomenal. You should hear his Howlin' Wolf impersonation; he can make your hair stand on end. I've heard people say he sounds just like Albert King or so-and-so. Well, if you really heard him do those people, he really does sound like them. If he wants to impersonate someone, he's got it down. But when he gets onstage, that's Robert Cray.
Eric Clapton, *Rolling Stone*, 1988

This version of 'Bad Influence' is rather polite, lifted by some great saxophone by Michael Brecker and a long guitar solo by Clapton.

'Walk Away' (Feldman, Detroit)
A very commercial song, 'Walk Away' sounds nothing like Eric Clapton. It was co-composed by Richard Feldman and Marcella Detroit (formerly Marcy Levy). This pair had provided 'Tangled in Love' for *Behind the Sun*. Its shimmering keyboard and gated drums place 'Walk Away' in the middle of the 1980s.

'Hung Up on Your Love' (Dozier)
Another Lamont Dozier composition–much tougher than many of the other songs on *August*. A funk bassline, a superbly catchy chorus, a strong vocal and

hardly any guitar are married to a startling prog rock interlude. Despite all of this, or perhaps because of it, 'Hung Up on Your Love' is a brilliant song.

'Take a Chance' (Clapton, East, Phillinganes)
A funky pop song showing the consummate skill of the band on these sessions. Of all the songs on *August*, this perhaps has the biggest Phil Collins stamp – the drum sound, popping bass, backing vocals and parping horns are straight from *No Jacket Required*. Considering this was written and recorded when someone who wasn't his wife was expecting his child, Clapton's lyrics are decidedly unapologetic.

> If I don't play around, how am I gonna have my fun?
> If I tried to settle down, would I be fooling anyone?

'Hold On' (Clapton, Collins)
Released as a single June 1987, B-side of 'Tearing Us Apart'

A weak song, dominated by Phil Collins' pounding drums. Eric doesn't sound convinced by the words he is singing, and there are so many post-production effects on the guitar that it almost disappears into the mix. Tina Turner sweetens the backing vocals.

'Miss You' (Clapton, Columby, Phillinganes)
Finally, a song with some muscle. 'Miss You' is a powerful, modern R & B song co-written by Eric and Greg Phillinganes with former Blood, Sweat and Tears drummer Bobby Columby. Columby and Phillinganes were old friends. With lots of chances for Eric to cut loose on guitar, contemporary live versions of 'Miss You' were simply superb, with Clapton pushed hard by an incomparable band.

'Holy Mother' (Bishop, Clapton)
Released as a single November 1987, highest chart placing: UK: 95.

'Holy Mother' is one of Eric Clapton's best, and most personal songs. It dates from mid-1984.

> While we were in Canada, playing at Maple Leaf Gardens in Toronto [on the Roger Waters tour], I hit a rock bottom, one of a series that would eventually lead me back to Hazelden. I had been drinking very heavily throughout the tour and had suffered one or two alcoholic breakdowns, like mini seizures. I just hit a wall of desperation. I was out on the road in a massive downward spiral with drink and drugs, I saw *Purple Rain* in a cinema in Canada. I had no idea who he was, it was like a bolt of lightning! In the middle of my depression, he was like a light in the darkness. It was like a moment of clarity when I saw the absolute squalidness of my life at that moment. I went back to my hotel,

and, surrounded by empty beer cans, I began to write 'Holy Mother', in which I asked for help from a divine source, a female that I couldn't even begin to identify. It came from deep in my heart as a sincere cry for help.

The song was co-written by Stephen Bishop, who had a solo hit with 'On and On' (1976) and wrote the US number one 'Separate Lives' for Phil Collins and Marilyn Martin. Eric Clapton played guitar on two songs on Bishop's first solo album *Careless* released in 1976 and two more on *Red Cab to Manhattan* (1980). Bishop, quoted at stephenbishop.com:

Phil Collins married his second wife, Jill, in [August] 1984 and I was invited to the wedding. So I went and stayed at Eric's. While I was there, Eric asked me if I wanted to work on this idea he had called 'Holy Mother'. I went upstairs to my room and started working on the idea – played what I had for him, and he worked on it later.

'Holy Mother' was released as the lead single from *August*, just scraping into the UK top 100.

'Behind the Mask' (Mosdell, Sakamoto, Jackson)
Released as a single January 1987, highest chart placing: UK: 15.

Eric Clapton's biggest UK hit single since 'I Shot the Sheriff' was written by Ryuichi Sakamoto and was originally recorded in 1979 by Sakamoto's Yellow Magic Orchestra, with lyrics by Japan-domiciled British lyricist Chris Mosdell. Michael Jackson wrote new lyrics, replacing most of Mosdell's, and recorded his own version during the sessions for *Thriller* (1981-1982). But this was not included on the world's best-selling album due to a royalty dispute. Jackson's keyboard player Greg Phillinganes recorded 'Behind the Mask' for his solo album *Pulse* (1985) – this might even be Jackson's demo version with new vocals and instrumentation. It's Phillinganes' version that forms the arrangement for Eric Clapton's recording – Phillinganes was, of course, a key contributor to *August,* and a Clapton band member in this period. A radically remixed version of Jackson's track, with extra overdubbed production was eventually released on the 2010 posthumous album *Michael*.

'Behind the Mask' is effortlessly commercial synthpop with a catchy melody, a dance-friendly beat, and Michael Jackson's obtuse lyrics. The single version is edited, chopping out most of Eric's guitar solo.

'Grand Illusion' (Farrell, Robbins, Stephenson)
Released March 1987, B-side of 'It's in the Way That You Use It'

'Grand Illusion', only initially available on the CD release of *August*, was written by the songwriting team of Van Stephenson, Dave Robbins and Bob

Farrell. Stephenson was an American singer-songwriter who scored three US *Billboard* Hot 100 hits between 1981-1984. Stephenson and co-composer Dave Robbins were the principal writers for the American country music group Restless Heart's debut album, released in 1985. Bob Farrell is one half of a husband-and-wife Contemporary Christian Music duo that recorded albums from about 1977 to 1991. Add this song's unlikely provenance to Phil Collins' thumping production and here's another song that sounds nothing like Eric Clapton. But Eric delivers a confident vocal and a melodic guitar solo. 'Grand Illusion' was covered by Donny Osmond in 1988.

Other Contemporary Tracks
'Wanna Make Love to You' (Williams)
Most likely dropped to make way for 'It's in the Way That You Use It', this powerful, sexy Jerry Lynn Williams song nevertheless formed part of Clapton's setlist in the series of concerts between completion of the sessions in Montserrat in May 1986 and the album's release in November. It's full of fiery guitar and is better than at least half the songs chosen for *August*. 'Wanna Make Love to You' can be heard on the 'Behind the Mask' CD single and the *Crossroads* box set. Bobby Womack also recorded this song for his album *Womagic*, released a few months before *August*, as did, amazingly, both Dr Feelgood and Johnny Hallyday.

'Lady of Verona' (Clapton)
A commercial song with hammering drums, a Phil Collins-sheen, and a driving guitar solo, this paean to Lory del Santo has lines such as 'I fell in love with a lady from Verona, she's just as sweet as she can be / All of her life she's been a loner. Because she likes to be free....' It is probably best that this stayed in the can. Hear it on YouTube.

'Walking the White Line' (unknown)
An unheard outtake from the *August* sessions, as reported by Marc Roberty in *The Complete Recording Sessions*. There is a track on a bootleg album called *August Session* that claims to be this, but who knows if it's genuine?

'It's My Life Baby' (Robey, Washington)
Recorded in August-September 1986 with the Big Town Playboys, a six-piece acoustic British rhythm and blues group. Although recorded by Junior Wells and Buddy Guy in 1966, the song is credited to Don Robey, an American music executive and producer who often claimed full or part-writing credits of tracks released on his record label. Eric's sluggish version was included in the Paul Newman/Tom Cruise film *The Color of Money* but is not on the soundtrack album. The Big Town Playboys would be the support act on Clapton's 1987 UK tour. The song would later be performed during the blues-only set at the Royal Albert Hall, February-March 1993.

'After Midnight' (Cale)

A new version of one of Eric's better-known covers, dating from summer 1987 at the Power Station. It was recorded for a Michelob commercial with Nathan East, Alan Clark and Andy Newmark. Eric to *Rolling Stone* in 1988:

> I was a practising alcoholic when I made that. By the time it came out, I was in treatment This was December of '87. I was actually in treatment in Minnesota when that came on the TV. I was in a room full of recovering alcoholics, myself being one of them, and everybody went, 'Is that you?' I said, 'Yep.' What was I going to say? It was me when I was drinking. I don't know if it was offered to me now whether I would do it. But then again, I'm not a preacher. I'm not one to say whether people should be drinking or not. Otherwise, I'd have to come down on all my mates, like Phil, who does it as well. I can only speak for myself. I don't drink anymore, and I'd rather not drink ever again.

'In the Air Tonight' (Collins)

Introduced as 'that song again' when performed as part of Eric Clapton's live set in 1986 by drummer Phil Collins. Clapton adds slabs of distorted guitar.

'Money for Nothing' (Knopfler, Sting)

Performed as part of Eric Clapton's live set in 1987 and 1988 by band-mate Mark Knopfler. Clapton joined Knopfler's Dire Straits for three gigs in June 1988, including the high-profile Nelson Mandela 70th Birthday Tribute. Clapton played the entirety of these sets and sang his own 'Wonderful Tonight' in a new arrangement.

Journeyman (1989)

Personnel:
Eric Clapton: lead vocals, guitar
Greg Phillinganes: keyboards, backing vocals
Richard Tee: keyboards
Nathan East: bass, backing vocals
Jim Keltner: drums
John Tropea: guitar on 'Hard Times'
Jeff Bova: keyboards and programming on 'Pretending', 'Anything for Your Love' and 'Breaking Point'
Alan Clark: keyboards on 'Pretending', 'Bad Love', 'Running on Faith', 'Run so Far', 'Old Love'
Robbie Kondor: keyboards and programming on 'Anything for Your Love', 'Hound Dog', 'No Alibis', 'Run So Far', 'Old Love'
Rob Mounsey: keyboards on 'Run So Far'
Robbie Kilgore: keyboards on 'Lead Me On'
Darryl Jones: bass on 'Run So Far'
Steve Ferrone: drums on 'Running on Faith', 'Hard Times', 'Lead Me On'
Carole Steele: percussion on 'Pretending', 'Running on Faith', 'No Alibis', 'Breaking Point', 'Lead Me On'
Gary Burton: vibraphone on 'Old Love'
Lani Groves: backing vocals on 'Running on Faith' and 'Run So Far'
Tawatha Agee and Vanessa Thomas: backing vocals on 'Breaking Point'
Hank Crawford, Ronnie Cuber, David 'Fathead' Newman, on Faddis and Lew Soloff: horns on 'Hard Times'
David Sanborn: alto saxophone on 'Breaking Point'
Robert Cray: guitar on 'Anything for Your Love', 'Hound Dog', 'Old Love', 'Before You Accuse Me'
George Harrison: guitar, backing vocals on 'Run So Far'
Cecil and Linda Womack: guitar, vocals on 'Lead Me On'
Chaka Khan: backing vocals on 'Pretending' and 'No Alibis'
Daryl Hall: backing vocals on 'No Alibis'
Rev. Timothy Wright Washington Temple Concert Choir on 'Running on Faith'.
Recorded March-April 1989 at the Power Station and Skyline Studios, New York.
Produced by Russ Titelman.
Personnel on 'Bad Love'
Eric Clapton: lead vocals, guitar
Phil Palmer: guitar
Alan Clark: keyboards
Pino Palladino: bass
Phil Collins: drums, backing vocals
Tessa Niles and Katie Kissoon: backing vocals
Recorded June 1989 at the Town House Studios, London. Produced by Phil Collins.
Released November 1989.
Highest chart positions: UK: 2, US: 16

Above: Eric in 1974, kicking off his solo career in his late 20s. **Inset:** Eric at the Royal Albert Hall in London in 2015.

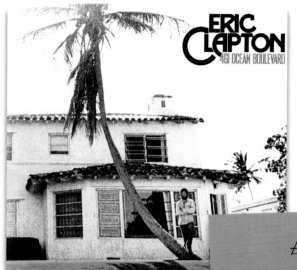

Left: Clapton stands outside (and on the cover of) *461 Ocean Boulevard*, his first studio album for almost four years. (*RSO*)

Right: *There's One In Every Crowd*. The quick follow-up to a top three album. It's not as good. (*RSO*)

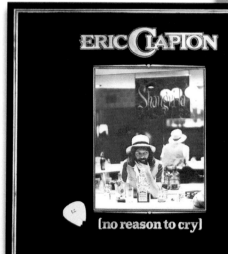

Left: Recorded with a host of famous friends, *No Reason to Cry* 'was made in Los Angeles with predictable results,' sniped *Rolling Stone*. 'The carefully sculpted, spiritual style of Clapton and his band has been replaced by a series of musical formulas.' (*RSO*)

E R I C   C L A P T O N

S L O W H A N D

Right: *Slowhand.* A terrific album from start to finish. (*RSO*)

Left: *Backless.* Every inch as good as *Slowhand.* (*RSO*)

Right: *Another Ticket.* Clapton's last album for RSO / Polydor, which includes a couple of forgotten gems. (*RSO*)

Left: Live on the *Old Grey Whistle Test* in 1977. Yvonne Elliman and a young Marcella 'Marcy Levy' Detroit are on the front line.

Right: Yvonne Elliman gets a solo spot during the *Old Grey Whistle Test* performance.

Left: Eric with George Terry on second guitar.

Right: Eric and moustache in the 'Bad Love' video in 1989.

Left: Keyboard player to the stars, Greg Phillinganes in the 'Bad Love' video.

Right: Bassist Nathan East in the 'Bad Love' video. Phil Collins was also in the 'live band' for the video.

Left: 1983's *Money and Cigarettes*. The fire of his earlier days starts to return. (*Warner Bros.*)

Right: *Behind The Sun* is three-quarters of a brilliant album. (*Warner Bros.*)

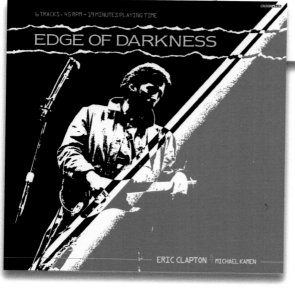

Left: The BAFTA-winning soundtrack to the BBC eco-thriller *Edge of Darkness*. A parallel career composing soundtracks had begun. (*BBC*)

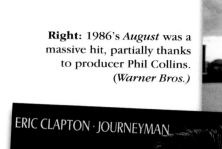

Right: 1986's *August* was a
massive hit, partially thanks
to producer Phil Collins.
(*Warner Bros.*)

Left: *Journeyman*. Clapton starts
to move away from AOR, beer
commercials and production
sheen. (*Reprise*)

Right: *Rush*. An obscure
soundtrack album heralds one of
Clapton's greatest songs in
'Tears in Heaven'. (*Reprise*)

Left: Eric on stage in 1990.

Right: *24 Nights* documented the 1990 and 1991 seasons at the Royal Albert Hall.

Left: On stage with long-time band members Andy Fairweather Low and Steve Gadd.

Right: Eric, still with rambling on his mind in 2001.

Left: Clapton plays Robert Johnson songs in Dallas with Doyle Bramhall II.

Right: Eric Rehearsing in 2004.

Left: *From The Cradle* was a thrilling return to the blues. Contemporary concerts were incendiary. (*Warner Bros.*)

Right: *Pilgrim* heralded a new sound with contemporary R & B and saw a new confidence in Clapton's singing. (*Reprise*)

Left: *Riding With B. B. King* - a classy collaboration with the blues legend. (*Reprise*)

Right: *Reptile*, Clapton's fourteenth solo album, features the astonishing 'Don't Let Me Be Lonely Tonight'. (*Reprise*)

Above and right: *Me and Mr. Johnson* and *Sessions for Robert J.* 'When he finds Satan on his doorstep in 'Me and the Devil Blues',' writes David Fricke, 'you can hear in Clapton's deep, scarred howl that he is confronting an old acquaintance'. (*Reprise*)

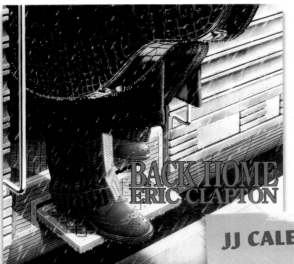

Left: *Back Home* - Clapton is sixty, sober and settled with a young family. (*Reprise*)

Right: Eric finally makes an album with his hero J.J. Cale. (*Reprise*)

Left: On 2010's *Clapton*, Eric revisits his roots. And not just the blues. (*Reprise*)

Right: *Old Sock* is another a stroll down memory lane, including pre-World War II songs like 'All of Me' and 'Goodnight Irene'. (*Surfdog / Polydor*)

Left: This all-star tribute album to the lately deceased J.J. Cale is tasteful, laid back and utterly professional. (*Surfdog*)

Right: *I Still Do* reunited Clapton with producer Glyn Johns. It's brilliant from start to finish. (*Surfdog*)

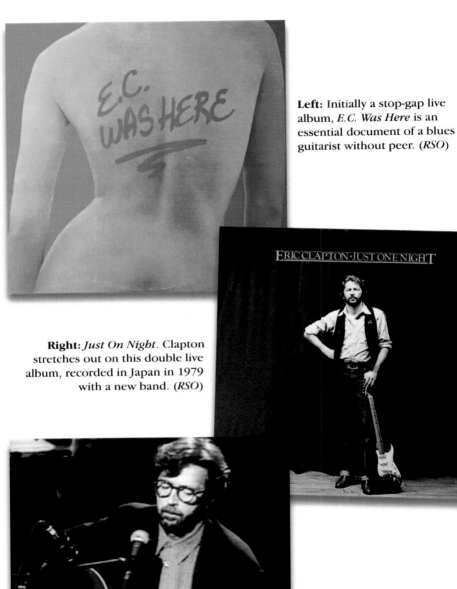

Left: Initially a stop-gap live album, *E.C. Was Here* is an essential document of a blues guitarist without peer. (*RSO*)

Right: *Just On Night*. Clapton stretches out on this double live album, recorded in Japan in 1979 with a new band. (*RSO*)

Left: 1992's *Unplugged* is Eric Clapton's biggest selling album. (*Reprise*)

Right: *Timepieces*. A big selling greatest hits album of songs from the 1970s. (*RSO*)

Left: The massive *Crossroads* box set signalled a new way for record companies to sell old songs. (*Polydor*)

Right: *Clapton Chronicles* gathers the hits from 1983 to 1999, including the huge sellers 'Tears in Heaven' and 'Change The World'. (*Reprise*)

Left: Eric recording at Olympic Studios in 2005.

Right: Just one of over two hundred times that Eric Clapton has performed at the Royal Albert Hall.

Left: *Slowhand at 70*. Eric celebrates his birthday at the Royal Albert Hall in 2015.

Live Aid, 'Behind the Mask', *August* and Ray Coleman's authorised biography (published in 1986) had helped raise and maintain the profile of Eric Clapton. Now in his early forties, he was seen as an elder stateman of the British rock music scene. Hour-long highlights of Clapton's 15 July 1986 concert in Birmingham were broadcast on Channel 4 and this includes a rare performance of 'White Room' with a solo that will melt your remote. Appearances at the televised Prince's Trust Rock Galas in 1986 and 1987 placed Clapton at the heart of two all-star bands with the likes of Paul McCartney, George Harrison, Mark Knopfler, Midge Ure, Elton John and, perhaps inevitably, Phil Collins. A six-part Radio One series called *Behind The Mask: The Eric Clapton Story* (July-August 1987) and a South Bank Show documentary (December 1987) ensured further publicity.

But still, Clapton struggled with alcohol dependency. Determined to be a father to his son Conor he returned to Hazelden in November 1987. This time he achieved and has retained, sobriety. Keeping busy, Clapton recorded contributions to three film and TV soundtracks in spring 1988. 'The Robbery' is an epic instrumental track recorded in March 1988 with composer Anne Dudley and included in *Buster*, which starred Eric's pal Phil Collins, whose exposure was by now reaching saturation point. The soundtrack album for Michael Serein's sports drama *Homeboy*, recorded in April 1988, includes fourteen bluesy instrumentals. The best of these are the elegant dobro-led 'Ruby' and a remarkable take on the Civil War tune 'Dixie'. The following month Clapton recorded fifty minutes of music for a TV documentary called *Peace in Our Time*. This marries blues guitar to orchestral backings and, despite its high quality, has never been commercially released outside the film's soundtrack. Likewise, the gentle soundtrack to Phillipe Mora's 1989 extraterrestrial horror film *Communion* includes eleven minutes of new music by Eric Clapton and Alan Clark. Again, this remains unreleased in its own right.

Finally, Clapton recorded a new version of the 'James Bond Theme' for the soundtrack for *The Living Daylights*, scored by his pal Michael Kamen. Legendary session guitarist Vic Flick, who had played the iconic guitar parts on the 1962 original, was also involved. Flick, interviewed by David J. Foster in 2009:

> It was a phone call out of the blue. Michael Kamen wanted a dark guitar sound to compliment the melody and extemporization Eric Clapton was going to do on their composition. So, knowing of my penchant for low-string guitar playing, he called me for the sessions. It was good to see Eric again after many years, and it was wonderful to work with those two gifted musicians. Eric played some amazing guitar on the track, and Michael worked out a fine arrangement. I did my thing with a counter theme in the low register.

A promotional video was filmed, but neither this, nor the audio recording, has ever leaked from the Bond producers' vaults.

Clapton's next solo album, *Journeyman*, would be recorded in New York with producer Russ Titelman who had achieved great success with albums for Randy Newman and Steve Winwood, as well as George Harrison's 1979 eponymous album, to which Clapton contributed. The core band for these sessions comprised Greg Phillinganes, Richard Tee, Nathan East and Jim Keltner... just about the best session musicians money and reputation can buy. Guests included Robert Cray on four tracks, Eric's old friend George Harrison on his own 'Run So Far', Womack and Womack on the relaxed duet 'Lead Me On', and vocal contributions from both Chaka Khan and Daryl Hall.

Journeyman balances the powerful pop-rock of his previous two albums – another six Jerry Lynn Williams songs makes eleven in total since 1985 – with covers of Ray Charles, Lieber & Stoller and Bo Diddley. It was a very successful album in the UK, hitting number two, his highest chart position since *Blind Faith* twenty years before. Ken Kelley said in *Ultimate Classic Rock* in April 2020:

> Clapton ended a rough decade with one of his best albums, a mix of 80s production polish and some mighty explosive guitar fireworks. Newly sober, he sounds in control of his career again. Even with a large guest list and slick period touches, *Journeyman* sounds like an era-defining statement by an artist ready to move on.

Journeyman was Eric Clapton's last album of (mostly) new material for nine years. By the time *Pilgrim* would be released in 1998, two huge hit singles in a new style would fundamentally change the course of his career.

'Pretending' (Williams)
Released as single, May 1990. Highest chart position: UK: 96, US: 55.

There's no doubting the commerciality of this Jerry Lynn Williams song. The instrumentation is given excessive studio treatment: Clapton's guitar is smothered in chorus effects, Jim Keltner sounds like he's playing in the bathroom down the hall, and future Celine Dion producer Jeff Bova adds bubbling synthesisers. It's all highly professional but with a welcome touch of swagger. The song worked well in concert and Clapton was fond enough of it to keep it as a semi-regular in his set through to the 2010s.

An early mix has a more live feel, pushed by rhythm guitar and piano rather than sequencer patterns. The introductory boogie-woogie piano was spliced on.

'Anything for Your Love' (Williams)
Busy production almost swamps a strong Eric Clapton vocal. The guitar break, however, is by-the-numbers, and has little drive. The chorus progression is great, but whose idea was the vocoder?

'Bad Love' (Clapton, Jones)
Released as single, January 1990. Highest chart position: UK: 25, US: 88.

'Bad Love' was recorded several weeks after the main Los Angeles sessions after Eric's record company once again wanted songs that could be released as singles. Pino Palladino's liquid fretless base introduces a furious guitar riff copped straight from 'Layla', arpeggios from 'Badge' and Phil Collins' thundering drums. Clapton remembered how the song came about on the Where's Eric? website:

> Warner Bros. wanted another 'Layla'. I thought, well, if you sit down and write a song in a formatted way, it's not so hard. You think, 'What was 'Layla' comprised of? A fiery intro modulated into the first verse and chorus with a riff around it. I had this stuff in my head, so I just juggled it around, and Mick Jones [of Foreigner] came in to help tidy up. He was the one who said, 'You should put a 'Badge' middle in there'. So, we did that. Although it sounds like a cold way of doing it, it actually took on its own life.

'Layla' it ain't, despite a guitar solo that flies above the bridge. 'Bad Love' won the award for Best Male Rock Vocal Performance at the 33rd Annual Grammy Awards (1990). The promo video sees Eric sporting a deeply unfortunate moustache.

'Running on Faith' (Williams)
The album's highlight – stripped of much of the production bluster and sung with real passion and soul, the gospel blues 'Running on Faith' is ambiguous enough to be interpreted as a religious affirmation. Or perhaps it's just a tribute to a more secular form of love. Either way, Clapton is 100% committed. The choir adds a genuine uplift to the coda. An earlier mix without the choir sounds simply empty. This outtake also has an electric lead guitar solo which was later replaced by dobro.

The definitive version is perhaps January 1992's live recording for *Unplugged*, played with tenderness and much feeling.

'Hard Times' (Charles)
A reverential and affectionate treatment of a Ray Charles song which has a timeless arrangement, a gritty blues guitar (the Cream-era Gibson 335), a rolling piano, parping horns, and a fat saxophone. New York jazz session guitarist John Tropea takes part but is not immediately audible. Unlike the more commercial songs on *Journeyman*, this performance hasn't aged at all: three minutes of bliss with Eric singing very well indeed.

'Hard Times', one of his Desert Island Discs in 1989, encouraged Clapton to head back to the blues, as he said at the time:

A lot of people have told me that their favourite track on the album is 'Hard Times'. It's very encouraging for me to know that I can make an album ... that will be comprised of entirely that kind of thing. I still feel protective towards the blues. It's a maligned art form and I get angry when I feel people are taking it too lightly. I go back to the blues because of its rawness. It's got more energy and vitality than anything I can think of. Most musicians who've been around will accept that the blues is the bottom line. It's always given me more out of life than sex, booze or any kick you can think of.

From *Eric Clapton: Uncensored and On The Record* (2012)

An alternative mix with a different lead vocal circulates amongst collectors.

'Hound Dog' (Leiber, Stoller)
A short, fun cover of the Big Mama Thornton song. Eric plays gritty electric slide and Robert Cray chimes in with some juicy fills. Eric:

Russ [Titelman] insisted that I do a version of 'Hound Dog', which turned out to be a great idea.

'No Alibis' (Williams)
Released as single, March 1990. Highest chart position: UK: 53.

Back to the pounding 80s production. 'No Alibis' is a commercial rock song with a hint of gospel, described by Marc Roberty as 'strong, anthem-like'. It certainly has a catchy chorus, and Clapton's guitar soars above. Guest vocalist Daryl Hall's counterpoint vocals in the second verse work particularly well. Chaka Chan adds harmony vocals in the chorus. An early mix presents the song with different lead guitar breaks, no Daryl Hall, and much of the production gloss removed. This reveals 'No Alibis' to be one of the better contemporary rock songs of this period.

'Run So Far' (Harrison)
Eric Clapton had played a major part in George Harrison's terrific *Cloud Nine*, released in 1987. George returns the favour here, donating 'Run So Far', which has a very mid-seventies feel, with acoustic guitars, Harrison-copyright slide, and George's sublime harmony vocals in the chorus. 'Run So Far' could almost be a Ronnie Lane song and provides some much-needed contrast on *Journeyman*. Harrison's version, with an identical arrangement, can be heard on 2002's *Brainwashed*.

'Old Love' (Clapton, Cray)
'Old Love', a mid-career highlight, the centrepiece of Journeyman, and one of Clapton's greatest songs, is a kiss-off to his by now ex-wife Pattie.

I can see your face, but I know that it's not real
Just an illusion caused by how I used to feel
Makes me so angry to know now that the flame will always burn
Never get over, know now that I'll never learn
Old love. Leave me alone.

Set to a slow-burning four-chord pattern, 'Old Love' is perhaps more poignant than bitter. Pattie told the *Guardian* in 2008 that she was hurt that Eric should write a song about such a sensitive subject. She said:

> The end of a relationship is a sad enough thing, but to then have Eric writing about it as well. It makes me more sad, I think, because I can't answer back.

'Old Love' is by some measure the best song on *Journeyman*. It was co-written with Robert Cray. Eric:

> We had a week of time together. And it was like, 'we've got to do something'. So I started playing the first part of the progression, which is A minor to F to G suspended to G, and then Robert started playing along with me. Robert came up with the turnaround, and then I just started writing the words. It was a perfect collaboration.

The guitar-playing is split 50:50. Cray takes the first solo (3:09-3:37, hear Eric say 'take me home, Bob' at the beginning), Clapton the second (3:38-4:03), and they trade licks as the song plays out, never overplaying, complementing each other with grace and style.

'Old Love' stayed in Eric's sets for years, and live performances were sometimes transcendent. Clapton and Cray performed the song together on David Sanborn's *Night Music* TV show in late 1989: Cray simply wipes the floor with Clapton. The thirteen-minute version on *24 Nights*, recorded in February 1991, is very good indeed, and the recording from June 1996 in London's Hyde Park is sublime. This can be enjoyed on the *Live in Hyde Park* DVD.

Upstart blues guitarist John Mayer has performed this in his own live sets and Eric's former bandmate Shaun Murphy recorded a fabulous version on *Flame Still Burns* (2020).

'Old Love' is a major song in the Clapton catalogue.

'Breaking Point' (Grebb, Williams)

'Breaking Point', the fifth Jerry Lynn Williams song on *Journeyman*, was co-written by Marty Grebb, a member of Bonnie Raitt's band for twenty-five years. It's a typical mid-paced rocker that could have come from any of the rock mafia of the late 1980s. It's at least two minutes too long.

An instrumental backing track without Clapton's lead guitar and vocals or David Sanborn's saxophone circulates with other *Journeyman* outtakes.

'Lead Me On' (Womack, Womack)
Eric Clapton:

> I wanted to get the Womacks because I thought it would be interesting to see
> how we would marry in the studio. It was just an experiment, really, and it
> worked incredibly well.

'Lead Me On' is a divine song: gentle, soulful, sexy, and emotional. Eric has
often turned to the classic R & B artists, and this unexpected combination
with Cecil and Linda Womack pays dividends. Vocals are shared between Eric
and Linda, Cecil plays some tough acoustic and adds harmonies, Eric adds
gentle guitar with taste and finesse. It's beautifully produced with strings that
complement rather than swamp.

An early mix has just Eric's lead guitar, Cecil's acoustic, Robbie Kilgore's
understated electric piano and the Womacks' vocals intertwining with
Clapton's easy delivery. The drums, percussion and strings are mixed out and
this gives this alternative version of 'Lead Me On' a remarkable intimacy.

'Before You Accuse Me' (McDaniel)
Clapton has riffed on this Bo Diddley song many times; two in-the-studio
versions from 1978 were released in 1999. This 1989 version started as a
simple Robert Cray/Jim Keltner in-studio jam. The resultant take was deemed
good enough to be added to *Journeyman*. 'Lead Me On' closes *Journeyman*
with a more organic, less produced sound which fits Clapton like a glove. Eric,
to *Guitar World* (2008):

> That was one of the very first records I ever heard. I think it was on an album
> that also featured 'Hey Bo Diddley', 'I'm a Man', 'Bring It to Jerome', and lots
> of other good things. It's a straight blues and can be played any way you like.

Other Contemporary Songs
'That Kind of Woman' (Harrison)
'That Kind of Woman' was one of several songs George Harrison offered to Eric
Clapton for the *Journeyman* album, along with 'Cheer Down', 'Run So Far' and
another unspecified title. Clapton duly recorded 'That Kind of Woman' in 1989
but chose not to include it on *Journeyman*. Gary Moore laid down his own
version later that year with Harrison on guitar and released this on *Still Got the
Blues* in March 1990.

Eric's version, meanwhile, was offered to Olivia Harrison, who had created
the Romanian Angel Appeal Foundation with Barbara Bach, Yoko Ono and
Linda McCartney in April 1990. The album *Nobody's Angel*, released in
November 1990, includes exclusive tracks by many artists.

'That Kind of Woman' has some typical Harrison chord changes and wry
lyrics. It's a lot of fun and deserves to be more widely known.

'Forever' (Williams)

An outtake from the sessions, written by Jerry Lynn Williams. It is perhaps too sluggish to have been a contender. Eric doesn't sound 100% committed.

'Don't Turn Your Back' (unknown)
'Something About You' (unknown)

Two songs included with other *Journeyman* outtakes. Both sound little more than demos with a guide vocal by someone who is not Eric Clapton. It sounds like Greg Phillinganes on 'Don't Turn Your Back' and, perhaps, Jerry Lynn Williams on 'Something About You'. It seems likely that E.C. does not take part in either of these, but they are included here for completeness.

'Murdoch's Men' (unknown)
'Higher Power' (unknown)

Two instrumental backing tracks included with other *Journeymen* outtakes. They are certainly complete songs with lots of potential, but without either vocals or lead instruments, they sound a long way from being finished. Eric Clapton's involvement is moot.

'This Kind of Life' (Croker)

Eric sings but does not play on 'This Kind of Life' from the self-titled 1989 album by Brendan Croker & The 5 O'Clock Shadows. Evidently, he had injured his hand playing cricket. 'This Kind of Life' is a relaxed and affectionate duet between Croker and Clapton. Their performances are very appealing and not so far from Croker's work with The Notting Hillbillies.

'Easy Lover' (Bailey, Collins, East)

A duet between Phil Collins and Nathan East performed as part of Eric Clapton's live set in 1989. Originally released as a single in 1984, where Collins duetted with Philip Bailey of Earth, Wind and Fire. It was a number one hit in the UK.

'Knockin' on Heaven's Door' (Dylan)

Randy Crawford's gorgeous take on 'Knockin' on Heaven's Door' was recorded for the soundtrack of *Lethal Weapon 2,* where it plays out over the closing credits. The song officially 'features Eric Clapton and David Sanborn' and is taut, jazz-tinged and very soulful. A second version used in the closing scene of the film has Eric on lead vocals and is much closer to Bob Dylan's original.

The single reached number 77 in a five-week UK chart run, September-October 1989.

'Border Song' (John, Taupin)

Two Rooms: Celebrating the Songs of Elton John and Bernie Taupin is one of the earliest multi-artist tribute albums. It was released in October 1991. It features Kate Bush, Sting, The Who, Jon Bon Jovi, Hall & Oates, Rod Stewart, Sinéad O'Connor and others. Clapton's contribution had been recorded at the Power Station in New York in May 1989 at the tail end of the *Journeyman* sessions. 'Border Song', originally from 1970's *Elton John*, is given a terrific New Orleans swagger that suits Eric's style perfectly. The arrangement leans heavily on Aretha Franklin's astounding version, also from 1970. Eric, interviewed by *The Washington Post* in 1991:

> I felt that I could identify with 'Border Song'. It reminds me of when I first met Elton–I could feel a way of doing it, with a horn section in a bluesy kind of way. Everything I have ever heard Elton and Bernie write has moved me at the time–moved me, encouraged me and inspired me–everything.

Rush (1992)

Personnel (on the songs):
Eric Clapton: guitar, vocals
Nathan East: bass
Randy Kerber: organ on 'Help Me Up'
Greg Phillinganes: piano on 'Help Me Up' and 'Don't Know Which Way to Go'
Chuck Leavell: piano and organ on 'Don't Know Which Way to Go'
Steve Ferrone: drums on 'Help Me Up' and 'Don't Know Which Way to Go'
Lenny Castro: percussion on 'Don't Know Which Way to Go' and 'Tears of Heaven'
Randy Kerber: organ, synthesizer on 'Help Me Up' and 'Tears of Heaven'
JayDee Maness: pedal steel on 'Tears of Heaven'
Gayle Levant: Celtic harp on 'Tears of Heaven'
Jimmy Bralower: drum machine on 'Tears of Heaven'
Bill Champlin, Vaneese Thomas, Jenni Muldaur, Lani Groves: background vocals on 'Help Me Up'
Buddy Guy: vocals, guitar on 'Don't Know Which Way to Go'
Recorded in late 1991. Produced by Russ Titelman. Released January 1992.
Highest chart position: US: 24

Eric Clapton would not release a full album of new songs between 1989's *Journeyman* and 1998's *Pilgrim*. He was far from idle, touring under his own name and, thrillingly, backing up his old friend George Harrison during a series of concerts in Japan in 1991. Guitarist Andy Fairweather Low joined Eric's band for the Harrison tour and has continued to work with Eric, on and off, since then.

During this period, Clapton recorded several instrumental soundtrack albums, including the third and fourth entries in the *Lethal Weapon* series and achieved two massive hit singles. The first of these hides on a soundtrack album for an American crime drama film directed by Lili Fini Zanuck, who would later make the *Life in 12 Bars* documentary. There are seven routine instrumentals and three songs.

'Help Me Up' (Clapton, Jennings)
'Help Me Up' deserves to be better known. The thumping drums and synthesisers of his previous few albums have gone, and, in their place, we have a more rootsy approach with clean guitars, Hammond organ and a great vocal.

'Don't Know Which Way to Go' (Dixon, Perkins)
A furious blues sung by Buddy Guy. Guy matches Clapton's guitar playing lick-for-lick. This is a re-working of a track recorded by Guy as early as 1963.

'Tears in Heaven' (Clapton, Jennings)
Released as a single, January 1992. Highest chart positions: UK: 5, US: 2.

There are many great guitarists, but very few who can write songs such as 'Tears in Heaven'. It's one of Eric Clapton's most famous songs and will always be associated with the tragic passing of Clapton's son Conor. The four-year-old had died after falling from the 53rd-floor window of a New York City apartment block belonging to a friend of Conor's mother, Lory Del Santo. 'He went in this room,' Del Santo said. 'As soon as I entered the room and I see the window. Where can he be?' Clapton was in New York at the time and was heading across town to pick up Conor for a day out. In a 2005 interview with *Mojo*, he said Conor's death 'threw me into ... a wobble'. Eric to A.B.C. News in 1992:

I almost subconsciously used music for myself as a healing agent, and lo and behold, it worked. I have got a great deal of happiness and a great deal of healing from music.

'Tears in Heaven' is one of several songs from this period that reflect Clapton's immediate emotions. 'I was trying to write [Jimmy Cliff's] 'Many Rivers to Cross' or [Bob Marley's] 'No Woman, No Cry,' he told *Rolling Stone* in 2017. 'It's the same chord progression. I don't know if I could express what I'm feeling in a blues, because a blues is at a level of anger and self-pity. And this was different.'

The timing was perfect because they needed a song about loss and I had plenty of them. 'Tears' was actually in a very embryonic stage when I was approached and I completed it for *Rush*. I needed the film to finish it because otherwise, I probably would have let it go. It was also a good opportunity for me to write about the loss of my son and have somewhere to put it, to channel it, because it didn't look like I was going into the studio in the near future. I really wanted to be able to say something about what happened to me and the opportunity that this movie presented me was excellent because it meant that I could write this song and express my feelings and have it come out quickly. After the song was done, I thought that it would be nice to put it out as a single as well.

Eric Clapton, quoted in *The Complete Guide To The Music Of Eric Clapton* (1995)

Clapton wrote this superior track with Will Jennings, who has written many famous songs for films such as 'Up Where We Belong' from *An Officer and a Gentleman* and 'My Heart Will Go On' from *Titanic*. Jennings wrote the lyrics to many of Steve Winwood's hits and has also worked with Joe Sample of The Crusaders: they collaborated on three albums for B.B. King. As Jennings recalled in an interview with songfacts.com:

Eric and I were engaged to write a song for a movie called *Rush*. We wrote a song called 'Help Me Up' for the end of the movie ... then Eric saw another place in the movie for [another] song and he said to me, 'I want to write a song about my boy'. Eric had the first verse of the song written, which, to me, is all the song, but he wanted me to write the rest of the verse lines and the release ('Time can bring you down, time can bend your knees ...'), even though I told him that it was so personal he should write everything himself. He told me that he had admired the work I did with Steve Winwood, and finally, there was nothing else but to do as he requested, despite the sensitivity of the subject. This is a song so personal and so sad that it is unique in my experience of writing songs.

'Tears in Heaven' was released as a single in January 1992, reaching number two in the US, number five in the UK and number one in Argentina, Brazil, Canada, Denmark, Iceland, Ireland, Japan, New Zealand and Poland. It won Record of the Year, Song of the Year, and Best Male Pop Vocal Performance at the 35th Annual Grammy Awards. In 2004, *Rolling Stone* ranked 'Tears in Heaven' as the 362nd greatest song of all time. Eric once more, speaking to Mike Hrano in 2001:

'Tears in Heaven' ... you could think that that would be a different song to want to go back to but, in actual fact, the whole sentiment of that song is ... joyful is the not the right word but ... emotionally it's very moving, and it's a quite human and vulnerable place to go. I think that's important. I think allowing an audience to experience the artist's vulnerability is probably the most valuable thing you can give them.

Other Contemporary Songs
'Signe' (Clapton)
A relaxed, Latin-tinged instrumental which opened Eric's *Unplugged* show and has seemingly never been performed before or since. The finger-picked nylon-string technique from 'Tears in Heaven' makes a reappearance here. Eric, quoted in *Guitar World* (2008):

['Signe'] was written on a boat of the same name last year. I was on holiday with my manager and we chartered a beautiful yacht. It was a difficult time in my life, and I was writing to heal myself. 'Signe' was the first thing I started to write. It's just a melody which I dedicated to and named after the boat.

This is an extremely difficult song to play, and yet Clapton makes it look effortless.

'Hey Hey' (Broonzy)
'Hey Hey' is a Big Bill Broonzy song, a straight acoustic country blues. Broonzy (1903-1958) was active from the 1920s, and 'Hey Hey' was one of his last

singles, released in 1953. He also wrote the more famous 'Key to the Highway'. Eric in 2008:

> 'Hey Hey' was probably the first blues song I ever heard. I used to play it in pubs when I was very young.

Clapton's version was part of his *Unplugged* set.

'Lonely Stranger' (Clapton)
A gentle song with a strong message, originally written for a film soundtrack. Eric, in 2008:

> I wrote that in Los Angeles while I was doing the score for *Rush,* and I was just very lonely in LA. I felt like an English exile trying to beat the odds. You can get a lot of very strange vibrations coming in from the outside and doing something with the film industry. I really wrote that song to try to kind of cheer myself up.

The lyrics are very personal. 'Some will say that I'm no good / Maybe I agree / Take a look then walk away / That's all right with me,' he sings. The *Unplugged* performance is enhanced by Chuck Leavell's understated piano, Andy Fairweather Low's trilling mandolin, and the gentle backing vocals from Katie Kissoon and Tessa Niles. The feel and arrangement of the mega-hit 'Change the World' owes a lot to this unheralded song.

'Layla' (Clapton, Gordon)
Released as a single, September 1992. Highest chart positions: UK: 45, US: 12.

The acoustic arrangement of Clapton's rock classic included here to note that the single release of this *Unplugged* track was a top twenty hit in the US. It's 'a dispassionate, snooze-worthy bossa nova version of his 1970 masterpiece', according to *People* magazine.

'Walkin' Blues' (House)
Although usually credited to Robert Johnson, 'Walking Blues' is a Son House song adapted by Johnson with elements of House's 'My Black Mama'. Clapton takes the arrangement one step further as he told *Guitar World*:

> I borrowed the guitar part from one of the first Muddy Waters songs I ever heard, called 'Feel Like Going Home', then I superimposed Robert Johnson's lyrics. It's sort of my simultaneous tribute to both of them. It's a piece I've played since I was 14, but I only recently decided to start singing it. All of my original heroes played the slide and bottleneck, so maybe it's something I'll get into again.

Clapton's solo performance, recorded for *Unplugged* and accompanying himself on dobro, is sublime.

'San Francisco Bay Blues' (Fuller)

Eric goes full-on skiffle for this *Unplugged* performance, with a rare use of 12-string acoustic and a unique solo on the kazoo. He told *Guitar World*:

> I've heard several versions of it, but the first one I heard was performed by Jesse Fuller, and it was Jesse Fuller as a one-man-band. He had two bass drums, a foot bass, harmonica, kazoos, and a great, big 12-string guitar. It was one of those songs he played in pubs to get free beer, so it's very accessible on a sing-along level.

In this vein, it's perhaps no surprise that Paul McCartney performed this same song in his own *Unplugged* set, recorded almost exactly one year before Clapton's.

'Malted Milk' (Johnson)

A very faithful rendition of one of Robert Johnson's classic blues songs, performed at the *Unplugged* show by Eric Clapton and Andy Fairweather Low. Eric, to *Guitar World*:

> 'Malted Milk' is a peculiar song. It's very ironic, because it's quite clear that it's not malted milk he's referring to throughout the song. It came from a period where Robert was changing his style, and it sounds to me like he came across Lonnie Johnson in his travels. There was a massive shift in his style of accompaniment and his style of singing. I've never approached this song before, and probably wouldn't have if I hadn't had this opportunity to try it out. It's a very beautiful song.

'Runaway Train' (John, Taupin, Romo)

A vocal duet with Elton John from the *Lethal Weapon 3* soundtrack and John's twenty-third album *The One*, released in June 1992. Eric and Elton performed three double-headliner dates at London's Wembley Stadium that month. 'Runaway Train' is booming pop-rock with two loud Clapton guitar solos. It was released as a single in July 1992 and reached number 31 in the UK.

'It's Probably Me' (Sting, Clapton, Kamen)

Eric gets co-performer credit on the original release of 'It's Probably Me', a top 30 UK single in 1992 and also, in a longer version, on the *Lethal Weapon 3* soundtrack. Eric plays nylon-strung acoustic and a tight electric guitar solo. Steve Gadd, David Sanborn and Michael Kamen also contribute. The version on Sting's *Ten Summoner's Tales* (1993) is a re-recording without any of these musicians.

'Fight (No Matter How Long)' (Gibb, Gibb, Gibb, English)

'Fight' comes from the soundtrack album to a series of animated shorts about a bunny cricket team based on a series of children's books by David English. 'Fight' was produced by the Bee Gees, who get artist co-credit here. It's a strong song – The Bee Gees' backing vocals suit Eric's singing and there is lots of loud lead guitar. The song was released on *The Bunbury Tails* album in October 1992, which is now a collector's item. This album also includes otherwise unavailable tracks by George Harrison, Elton John and The Bee Gees.

From the Cradle (1994)

Personnel:
Eric Clapton: lead vocals, guitar
Andy Fairweather Low: guitar
Chris Stainton: keyboards
Dave Bronze: bass
Jim Keltner: drums
Jerry Portnoy: harmonica
Simon Clarke: baritone saxophone
Tim Sanders: tenor saxophone
Roddy Lorimer: trumpet
Richie Hayward: percussion on 'How Long Blues'
Recorded in 1994 at Olympic Studios, Barnes. Produced by Eric Clapton and Russ
Titelman. Released September 1994.
Highest chart positions: UK: 1, US: 1

> I would like to make a blues album. That will probably come after my next solo
> album, which I think will be a commercial venture again.
> **Eric in 1986.**

**True to his word, Eric's setlist from early 1993 was almost totally comprised of
classic blues songs, many of which he'd never performed live before. Eric:**

> Having opened the door to my true musical tastes with *Unplugged,* I decided
> it was time to say thank you to the blues and to the players and singers who
> had inspired me so much throughout my life, people like Elmore James,
> Muddy Waters, Jimmie Rodgers and Robert Johnson. I went into the studio
> with the approach that everything would be recorded live, and having chosen
> the songs, we would play them as much like the original versions as possible,
> even down to the key they were played in. It was great fun, and I loved every
> minute of it. It was what I had always wanted to do.

**His band comprised long-time associates Andy Fairweather Low and Chris
Stainton with Jerry Portnoy (harmonica), Duck Dunn (bass) and Little Feat's
Richie Hayward (drums). Dunn was replaced at the 1994 recording sessions
by Dave Bronze, who became Eric's full-time bassist until 1997. Hayward plays
percussion on one track, but the main drum duties fell to Jim Keltner. With the
exception of two overdubs, the album was performed live. As Eric said in the
From The Cradle tour programme:**

> We come in at about 11.30am and we work till four or five. It's like playing a
> very long concert. And there's no hanging around. We don't sit around and
> deliberate whether anyone should overdub. We get to the bones of the matter
> straight away, and then when we're tired, we stop.

The album's title comes from the last line of a four-line poem written by Clapton: 'All along this path I tread / My heart betrays my weary head / With nothing but my love to save / From the cradle to the grave.'

The success of *Journeyman* and *Unplugged*–the latter is the biggest selling album of Clapton's career–pushed *From the Cradle* to the top of the UK album charts for a single week immediately upon its release. It is Clapton's only UK number one solo album to date and was his first top ten in America since *Another Ticket* in 1981. It won the Grammy for Best Traditional Blues Album and was nominated for Album of the Year. Unfortunately, and despite a few notable exceptions, the finished album lacks much of the fire of his blues performances in concert. Like Richard Thompson's *1000 Years of Popular Music*, *From the Cradle* is worthy but not engaging end-to-end; a history lecture with sparks of genius rather than an album to play regularly all the way through.

Sixteen songs and an hour in length, *From the Cradle* is perhaps twenty minutes or four songs too long. Individual songs such as 'Third Degree', 'Reconsider Baby', 'Five Long Years', 'I'm Tore Down' and 'Driftin' Blues' are excellent, but overall the album has a little too much filler.

Clapton and his band–now with Andy Newmark on drums and a three-piece horn section–appeared on *Saturday Night Live* to promote *From the Cradle*. The performances of 'Five Long Years' and 'Tore Down' were arguably more powerful than the studio versions. This is borne out by recordings of the subsequent concert tour when Clapton played some of the best shows of his career. A 90-minute film of performances at The Fillmore in November 1994, *Nothing but the Blues*, was released in June 1995 in the United States via the PBS broadcasting companies around the country. It shows Eric's commitment to this phase of his career.

'Blues Before Sunrise' (Carr)

Written by American blues singer and pianist Leroy Carr, recorded and released by Carr and guitarist Scrapper Blackwell in 1934. Clapton's oddly pedestrian version was inspired by Elmore James's 1955 rendition of the song. The slide guitar is down and dirty, but Clapton's vocals sound forced.

'Third Degree' (Boyd, Dixon)

A slow-burning blues first recorded in 1953 by Eddie Boyd. Clapton's version is very faithful to the original with a live feel – he even wanders away from the mike at one point. As Eric told writer Marc Roberty:

> I was actually trying as hard as I could to try and replicate the original recordings. But it still came out as me, which is the beauty of the whole exercise ... It's almost like I'm just leaving John Mayall now and I'm producing my own blues band. And it's taken me 30 years of meandering the back streets to get there. We did Eddie Boyd's song, 'Third Degree', which just blew

everyone away for a little while. We listened to his recording of it, and we went out there and we did it in two takes, it was just easy.

Clapton's mastery of the electric blues guitar is evident on tracks such as this, and Chris Stainton finally gets to shine on piano.

'Reconsider Baby' (Fulson)

A great song choice here, originally recorded by Lowell Fulson in 1954. 'Reconsider Baby' gives Clapton the chance to exercise not only his vocal chops – it's right in his range – but also play tribute to Fulson's fluid blues guitar playing. He also tips his hat to Freddie King's 1972 arrangement, copping the lead guitar almost note for note. This is a good thing. Clapton played this song on *Later With Jools Holland* in 1995, spanking his Cream-era Gibson in a quite remarkable performance with Holland's huge R'n'B Orchestra. Delicious. Track down Elvis Presley's 1960 version for another excellent variant.

'Hoochie Coochie Man' (Dixon)

Do we really need another version of 'Hoochie Coochie Man', which employs probably the most famous blues lick ever written? The song was penned by Willie Dixon and originally recorded by Muddy Waters in 1954. Clapton's recording is a pumped-up rearrangement of the version he played with John Mayall's Bluesbreakers in 1965. It misses Waters' stately grace. Eric, in his tour programme:

> 'Hoochie Coochie Man' is like the crown jewels, isn't it? I mean, don't go near this song, don't anybody go near this song. Why am I doing it? It's like in the lion's den with this one.

Perhaps 'I Feel Like Going Home' (one of Eric's *Desert Island Discs*), 'Just Can't Be Satisfied' or 'Long Distance Call' (performed live in 1993) would have served Waters' memory better?

'Five Long Years' (Boyd)

A tough rendition of Buddy Guy's arrangement of a 1949 song by Eddie Boyd, also performed by Eric during his time with The Yardbirds and released in 1964 on *Five Live Yardbirds*.

This new version of 'Five Long Years' has a truly astonishing guitar solo – Eric plays like a man possessed, and it's one of the best of his career.

'I'm Tore Down' (Thompson)

Originally performed by Freddie King in 1961 and credited to King's pianist Sonny Thompson. Clapton's early career was massively influenced by King – right down to his choice of Gibson ES-335 guitar and open-handed picking. Eric, quoted in *Ultimate Guitar* (2019):

Of all the people I've played with, the most stimulating in an onstage situation was Freddie King. He could be pretty mean but subtle with it. He'd make you feel at home and then tear you to pieces ... He taught me just about everything I needed to know ... when and when not to make a stand ... when and when not to show your hand. . . and most important of all ... how to make love to a guitar.

Clapton uses an arrangement close to King's original, including the falsetto vocal phrases and note-for-note guitar fills. Live versions in 1994-1995 were practically combustible.

'How Long Blues' (Carr)
A second Leroy Carr song, dating from 1928, which was a progenitor to the more famous 'Sitting on the Top of the World' and 'Come On in My Kitchen'. Eric Clapton's version keeps the honky-tonk piano from the original, switches acoustic guitar for some welcome dobro, and adds harmonica, percussion, and a great lead vocal. This was the opening song on his 1993 blues-only concerts.

'Goin' Away Baby' (Lane)
'Goin' Away Baby' was written by Jimmy Rogers (not the Singing Brakeman) and credited to his real name, Jay A Lane. Rogers was the guitar player in Muddy Waters' first electric band, formed in 1947. Clapton's version is harder, with a Chicago blues strut driven by Jerry Portnoy's best Little Walter impression.

'Blues Leave Me Alone' (Lane)
Another Jimmy Rogers song with blasting harmonica, taken at a faster pace than Rogers', but otherwise a fair copy.

'Sinner's Prayer' (Glenn, Fulson)
'Sinner's Prayer' was first released by Lowell Fulson in 1950, but it's Ray Charles' 1953 version that inspires Clapton here. There's some hot guitar and a passionate vocal from Eric.

'Motherless Child' (Hicks)
Released as single, 1994. Highest chart positions: UK: 63, US: did not chart.

First recorded as 'Motherless Chile Blues' as early as 1927 by the song's author Robert 'Barbecue Bob' Hicks (this is worth tracking down as it's quite gorgeous), Eric Clapton's version is closely and respectfully modelled on the original; heartfelt and very beautiful. A contrast from the loud electric blues elsewhere on *From the Cradle*, 'Motherless Child' was performed in the acoustic portion of the *Nothing but the Blues* tour with Eric on 12-string.

'It Hurts Me Too' (London)

Elmore James provides the template for this Mel London song, made famous by Tampa Red in 1940. 'It Hurts Me Too' was previously recorded by Clapton in 1974, and twenty years later, this new version adds a strong, rhythmic backing and loud slide guitar.

'Someday After a While (You'll Be Sorry)' (King, Thompson)

Written and recorded by Freddie King in 1964, Clapton drops the tempo and pumps up the guitar on this excellent, powerful blues tune. When the solo guitar and horns kick in, the listener is lifted out of their seat; the playing here is remarkable.

'Standin' Round Crying' (Morganfield)

'Standin' Round Crying' is one of Muddy Waters' best-known songs, first released in 1952 on *Muddy Waters and His Guitar*. It's a tough, slow blues, dominated by Little Walter's blasting blues harmonica. The version for *From the Cradle* is practically a facsimile, reverential and professionally executed, but not adding anything new. Clapton and Waters performed the song together in 1978. Eric and Pete Townshend performed an acoustic version of this song in October 1989 for the BBC TV programme *Saturday Matters*.

'Driftin'' (Brown, Moore, Williams)

Part of Eric's live set in the 1970s–there's a version on *EC Was Here*–'Driftin'' was first recorded by The Three Blazers in 1945, where it has piano, brushed drums, double bass and jazzy electric guitar. Clapton resets it here as a country blues; solo acoustic guitar, perfectly performed with heart and skill. Two live versions which really need to be tracked down are from 2015, acoustic and outstanding, available on the *Slowhand at 70* DVD, and an astonishing electric workout on the *Nothing But the Blues* film.

'Groaning the Blues' (Dixon)

Another Willie Dixon song, released by Otis Rush in 1957. Clapton supercharges the original with a very long and very good guitar solo.

> The album's pièce de résistance. Eric has simply not played better at any time in his long and illustrious career. Here is a man clearly enjoying himself and playing what he chooses.
> Marc Roberty, *Eric Clapton–The Complete Guide to His Music* (2005)

Other Contemporary Songs

'32-20 Blues' (Johnson)

Released as single, B-side of 'Motherless Child'.

This is an up-beat Robert Johnson song, recorded during Eric's residency at the Royal Albert Hall in February-March 1993. It includes snatches of Howlin'

Wolf's 'Forty-Four Blues' for good measure. Eric would record a studio version in 2004.

'Baby Don't You Hear Me Calling' (Fulson)
A furious take on a Lowell Fulson song, only performed a few times in 1993.
   Note that online sources credit this to Alvin Lee of Ten Years After. Ten Years After did perform a song called 'Hear Me Calling', but it's not this one.

'Chicago Breakdown' (Merriweather)
A Big Maceo Merriweather song performed during the blues-only set at the Royal Albert Hall, February-March 1993.

'Tell Me Mama' (Jacobs)
Almost rockabilly, this is a 1953 Little Walter song with blasting harmonica. It was part of Eric's 1993 blues sets.

'Juke' (Jacobs)
A harmonica instrumental recorded by Little Walter Jacobs in 1952 and performed during the blues-only set at the Royal Albert Hall, February-March 1993 as a showcase for Jerry Portnoy.

'Coming Home' (James)
An Elmore James song from 1957 performed during the blues-only set at the Royal Albert Hall, February-March 1993.

'You've Got To Love Her With a Feeling' (King)
A Freddie King song, the A-side of a single with 'Have You Ever Loved a Woman?' on the flip. It was performed during the blues-only set at the Royal Albert Hall, February-March 1993.

'Let Me Love You, Baby' (Dixon)
'Let Me Love You, Baby' was written by Willie Dixon and recorded by Buddy Guy in 1961. Eric was probably also familiar with Stevie Ray Vaughan's version from *In Step* (1989). Either way, this was one of over a dozen songs performed in 1993-1994 that Eric has never formally recorded.
   Clapton and Guy performed the song with B. B. King in 2005 at the Rock and Roll Hall of Fame live concert, following Guy's induction.

'Forty-Four Blues' (Sykes)
A blues standard first recorded by Roosevelt Sykes in 1929. Eric played the Howlin' Wolf arrangement on his 1993 and 1994 tours.

'Ain't Nobody's Business if I Do' (Grainger, Robbins)
Part of Eric's live set in 1993-1994, this blues song from the 1920s was

recorded by Bessie Smith, although it's Jimmy Witherspoon's 1949 recording that most likely inspired Clapton's cover.

'Kidman Blues' (Jones)
Another 1920s blues, recorded by Bertha 'Chippie' Hill in 1925 and later by Big Maceo Merriweather. This song was part of Eric's live set in 1993-1994. A version of 'Kidman Blues' can be heard on the 2011 album *Play the Blues: Live From Jazz at Lincoln Center* by Wynton Marsalis and Eric Clapton.

'Every Day I Have the Blues' (Memphis Slim)
Although not written by him, 'Every Day I Have the Blues' is most associated with B.B. King: the song opens his classic 1965 album *Live at the Regal*. Eric performed the song on some dates on the second leg of the *Nothing but the Blues* tour.

'I Can't Judge Nobody' (Jackson, Thompson)
A cover of a 1960 single by Otis 'Smokey' Smothers performed on some dates of the *Nothing but the Blues* tour.

'I'm Gonna Cut Your Head, Mama' (Harris)
A raw blues song performed on tour in 1995. It was written and recorded by Homer Harris, who was one of the first Mississippi musicians to move to Chicago. He is known to have recorded just three songs, all with Muddy Waters, including this one dating from 1946.

'Mississippi Blues' (Brown)
The Music Maker Relief Foundation was founded in 1994 by folklorist Tim Duffy, 'to preserve the musical traditions of the South by directly supporting the musicians who make it'. Duffy recalls meeting Eric Clapton in late 1995 at whereseric.com:

> Eric noticed the 1930 Martin 00-18 sitting in the corner. When Eric began to play, it was spellbinding, and among the most amazing musical moments of my life. I picked up my guitar and quickly tuned it a half-step up to match his and began to play some backup guitar licks.

The recording is clearly off-the-cuff but showcases the country blues side of Clapton's playing to great effect. It was released in 2019 on *Blues Muse*, a various artists album that raises funds for the Music Maker Relief Foundation, and can be heard on Soundcloud.

'Got My Mojo Working' (Morganfield)
Muddy Waters' signature song performed on some dates of the *From the Cradle* tour, and regularly in 2008.

'St James Infirmary' (traditional)

Performed by Clapton with Dr John at their *Duets* show for VH1, recorded at the Roseland Ballroom in New York on 9 May 1996. Their version leans heavily on the Bobby 'Blue' Bland recording of 1961.

'Stone Free' (Hendrix)

From *Stone Free: A Tribute to Jimi Hendrix*, released in November 1993. This brilliant rarity sounds like a lost Cream outtake. Eric's singing and playing are superlative, here. If anyone doubts that, on his day, Clapton could match Hendrix note-for-note, then play them this. Clapton would add an incendiary 'Stone Free' to his live set in 1993-1994.

'The Burning of the Midnight Lamp' (Hendrix)

Eric's admiration for Jimi Hendrix is borne out in this wah-wah heavy rock-soul arrangement of Hendrix's introspective and melancholic song. Eric's amazing solo will give you goosebumps. Recorded in 1993, this version would not be released until 2004 on *Power of Soul: A Tribute to Jimi Hendrix*. It was performed a few times as part of Eric's set in autumn 1993.

'You Must Believe Me' (Mayfield)

'You Must Believe Me' is a sensational song first released by The Impressions in 1964. Clapton's robust, bluesier version is included on the terrific album *A Tribute to Curtis Mayfield*, released in February 1994 and bought by your author at a flea market in Drøbak, Norway, in 2019. Nile Rodgers is on second guitar; Eric on sensational lead vocals.

'Love Can Build a Bridge' (Judd, Overstreet, Jarvis)

A charity single, released as the official 1995 fundraising song for Comic Relief. Originally recorded by The Judds, it's sung here by Cher, Chrissie Hynde and Neneh Cherry. Although Clapton does not sing on this–he adds some trademark soloing in the central section–he is officially credited as a featured artist and appears in the video. A UK number one for a week in March 1995, this is Eric Clapton's only chart-topping single in his home country. It was thirty years, almost exactly, since his first chart entry with 'For Your Love'.

'Change the World' (Sims, Kennedy, Kirkpatrick)

Released as single, July 1996. Highest chart positions: UK: 18, US: 5.

Clapton's biggest latter-day hit single was recorded for the soundtrack of the 1996 film *Phenomenon*. It won Record of the Year and Best Male Pop Vocal Performance at the 39th Annual Grammy Awards. It was brought to Eric Clapton by Robbie Robertson, who was producing the soundtrack for *Phenomenon*. Co-writer Gordon Kennedy told the story of this song in an interview with *American Songwriter* magazine.

'Change the World' was a song written over the course of a year by Tommy Sims, Wayne Kirkpatrick, and myself. Wayne and I were recording some demos one day [in 1991], three of which wound up on Garth Brooks' *Chris Gaines* CD [1999, including the top five hit 'Lost in You']. During that session, Tommy was there playing bass, and played us the nugget of an idea he had, wondering if it might be something that would work for the sound we were doing. Wayne would ask him some months later for a tape of the idea so he could work on it. He wrote the lyrics to the chorus, and all but one line of the second verse. Then, it went dormant for a time before I asked Wayne about its progress. I finished writing the music and dictated lyrics into a little handheld recorder. I went into the studio and [recorded] a finished demo, the one Clapton heard later ... None of the three of us were together when we wrote the song.

'Change the World' builds on the template of songs like 'Lonely Stranger' and 'Tears in Heaven'. It's soulful, catchy folk-pop, produced by Kenneth 'Babyface' Edmonds, who had worked with Whitney Houston, Boyz II Men, Brandy, Mary J Blige and Usher, amongst others. Eric, in conversation with *Mojo* magazine (2013):

When I heard Tommy Sims demo, I could hear Paul McCartney doing that, so I needed to, with greatest respect to Paul, take that and put it somewhere black. So I asked Babyface, who, even though he may not be aware of it, gave it the blues thing. Babyface was one of those great catalysts for me. I'd seen him on TV doing his thing with acoustic guitar and I was thinking: 'this is a guy who's in the R'n'B world, he's a producer and yet he knows how to get that minimal thing and make a small sound really powerful.' And when I heard ['Change The World'], I put it on in my car and was driving around listening to it about 200 times without stopping. And I just knew it was a hit. And there's only one guy I knew that would make it absolutely right and that was Babyface.

The track was recorded in London and Los Angeles with John Robinson (drums), Dean Parks and Michael Thompson (guitar), Luis Conte (percussion), and old friends Nathan East and Greg Phillinganes. Babyface's smooth backing vocals are very evident in the chorus. Eric's performance, though, is still rooted in the blues, as he told *Mojo*:

The first two lines I play on that song on the acoustic guitar are lines I quote wherever I can. They come from the beginning of 'Mannish Boy' by Muddy Waters. On every record, I make where I think, 'this has got a chance of doing well', I make sure I pay my dues. It has to have one foot in the blues, even if it's subtly disguised.

There is an instrumental version of 'Change the World' on the CD single. It was first recorded by Wynona Judd and released on her February 1996 album,

Revelations, about four months before Eric Clapton's. Judd's has a faster tempo and a country twang. Clapton and Babyface perform the song together on *MTV Unplugged NYC 1997*.

'Danny Boy' (Weatherly)
More accurately, this is 'Londonderry Air', a traditional Irish instrumental folk ballad. It was recorded for a fifty-minute PBS documentary about 'Danny Boy' made by the team behind The Beatles' *Anthology* series. *In Sunshine or in Shadow* included musical interpretations and interviews with Shane McGowan, Marianne Faithfull, Sinéad O'Connor, Eric Clapton and Van Morrison. Eric was filmed performing the piece on nylon-strung acoustic guitar in Olympic Studios, presumably during the sessions for *From the Cradle*. It was released in 1996 on the 'Change the World' CD single, a worthwhile addition to Clapton's similar instrumental work for film soundtracks.

'Ruthie' (Clapton)
Eric Clapton performed at eleven European jazz festivals in July 1997 as part of the band Legends. And Legends they were: Steve Gadd, Marcus Miller, David Sanborn and Joe Sample are formidable musicians. Clapton had to be on his best form to keep up with a band of this calibre. They performed mostly instrumental pieces by Miller and Sanborn, but Clapton was able to add some pure blues such as 'Third Degree' and 'Every Day I Have the Blues', and yet another arrangement of 'Layla'.

Their performance at the Montreux Jazz Festival has been released on DVD. It's a 'must-watch' performance and includes an otherwise unavailable Clapton instrumental called 'Ruthie', named for his first daughter. It's a beautiful composition, brilliantly played despite a rare bum note from Eric.

An acoustic guitar/piano in-the-studio version of 'Ruthie' is in circulation. Its provenance is uncertain.

'Nil by Mouth' (Clapton)
A gentle, bluesy instrumental, the theme music to Gary Oldman's hard-hitting social drama, from 1998. Clapton's soundtrack has never officially been released.

Pilgrim (1998)

Personnel:
Eric Clapton: lead vocals, guitar
Simon Climie: keyboards and programming
Paul Waller: drum programming
Chyna Whyne: backing vocals
Andy Fairweather Low: guitar on 'My Father's Eyes'
Joe Sample: acoustic piano on 'My Father's Eyes' and 'You Were There'
Chris Stainton: Hammond organ on 'My Father's Eyes' and 'You Were There'
Paul Carrack: Hammond organ on 'Pilgrim', 'One Chance', 'Going Down Slow',
'Sick and Tired' and 'She's Gone', Wurlitzer electric piano on 'Going Down Slow'
Greg Phillinganes: keyboards on 'Broken Hearted' and 'Needs His Woman'
Nathan East: bass on 'My Father's Eyes', 'Broken Hearted', 'Circus', 'Fall Like Rain',
'Needs His Woman'
Luís Jardim: bass on 'River of Tears', percussion on 'River of Tears' and 'Born in
Time'
Pino Palladino: bass on 'One Chance', 'Going Down Slow', 'Born in Time' and
'She's Gone'
Dave Bronze: bass on 'You Were There'
Steve Gadd: drums on 'My Father's Eyes', 'Broken Hearted', 'She's Gone' and 'You
Were There'
Paul Brady: tin whistle and backing vocals on 'Broken Hearted'
Kenneth 'Babyface' Edmonds: backing vocals on 'Born in Time'
Tony Rich: backing vocals on 'Needs His Woman'
Recorded in 1997 at Olympic Studios, Barnes and Ocean Way Recording, Los
Angeles. Produced by Eric Clapton and Simon Climie. Released March 1998.
Highest chart positions: UK: 3, US: 4

**With the pure blues out of his system by the end of 1996, Eric Clapton toured
Europe in summer 1997 with jazzers David Sanborn, Joe Sample, Marcus
Miller and Steve Gadd in a mostly instrumental set that enlightened as much
as entertained. The band name Legends seems entirely appropriate. A Far East
tour that autumn with his own band (Sample and Gadd now hired hands)
reverted to a greatest hits set with a sprinkling of new songs, newly recorded
for his first album of original material since 1989.**

**_Pilgrim_ initiates the next phase of Eric Clapton's career: the first of his
collaborations with Simon Climie. Eric:**

I had written some songs I needed to finish and realized these had to be
done before I could feel completely at peace with myself. For this, I turned
for help to Simon Climie. We had met at Olympic Studios, and though I knew
him best as a songwriter and one-half of the group Climie Fisher, I also knew
he was producing modern R'n'B records, so it seemed for me like a natural
progression.

Climie Fisher was active between 1986 and 1990. Vocalist Climie, co-writer of the Aretha Franklin/George Michael classic 'I Knew You Were Waiting (For Me)', had met keyboard player Rob Fisher at Abbey Road Studios when they were both employed as session musicians. Their 1987 single 'Love Changes (Everything)' was a number two hit in the UK.

Clapton and Climie first worked together in 1996, composing music for a Giorgio Armani Fashion Show. This was expanded into a full album, *Retail Therapy*, released in March 1997 under the name TDF. *Retail Therapy* mixes trip-hop, techno, modern R'n'B, blues licks and ambient new age music – it is quite unlike anything else in Clapton's back catalogue and twenty-plus years on, it remains a fascinating oddity. But Climie's working methods chimed with Eric Clapton and the two musicians would collaborate on six more-traditional albums between 1997 and 2006: *Pilgrim*, *Reptile*, *Riding with the King*, *Me and Mr Johnson*, *Back Home* and *The Road to Escondido*.

Encouraged by Climie, Clapton wrote or co-wrote the majority of songs on *Pilgrim*: twelve out of fourteen. The majority of the basic tracks were recorded by Climie, Clapton and Climie's frequent collaborator Paul Waller. Many familiar musicians add to the mix: bass from Nathan East, Pino Palladino and Dave Bronze, Andy Fairweather Low on 'My Father's Eyes', Greg Phillinganes, Joe Sample and Chris Stainton on two tracks each, and Steve Gadd on four.

An important new face at these sessions was Paul Carrack, former front man of Ace, and co-vocalist in Mike + The Mechanics between 1985 and 2004. Carrack played Hammond organ on five songs and would join Clapton's touring band in 2013. Guests include Irish musician Paul Brady, who plays tin whistle on 'Broken Hearted', Kenneth 'Babyface' Edmonds, who provides backing vocals on 'Born in Time', and contemporary R & B singer Tony Rich who adds backing vocals to 'Needs His Woman'.

Pilgrim is a sad album, as Eric explained to Loudersound.com in 2016:

Well, that was my brief to the other musicians. I don't know if it was the brief to myself. I was trying to give them a map [laughs]. Did I achieve it? Almost.

Eric Clapton had once again taken a sharp turn in his musical style. Much of *Pilgrim* is contemporary soul-pop. Critical response was mixed. *People* magazine in March 1998 wrote:

Pilgrim is one long, slow slog, interrupted by only two or three up-tempo tunes. Listening is like sitting through a film you much admire but fervently wish would hurry up and end.

Natalie Nichols in the *LA Times* wanted 'a bit more … attitude, and fewer schmaltzy ballads.' David Wild in *Rolling Stone* wrote:

Pilgrim will not thrill those looking for *From the Cradle II* – most of this state-of-the-charts album sounds absolutely nothing like any record Muddy Waters ever made. But it's still a blues album in the sense that it captures the sound of a man trying to tame hellhounds from within and without. In the end, *Pilgrim* is not purely anything, except purely moving.

Individually the songs have aged well, but, as with *From the Cradle*, *Pilgrim* is perhaps over-long. It includes fourteen reflective and introspective songs, and at seventy-five minutes, *Pilgrim* is around the same running time as *Layla and Other Assorted Love Songs*.

The *Pilgrim* tour band comprised Andy Fairweather Low, Nathan East, and Katie Kissoon, with guitarist Alan Darby (a touring session musician with Van Morrison, Robert Palmer, Asia, Alannah Myles, Bonnie Tyler and Neneh Cherry and others), versatile keyboard players Tim Carmon and Kenneth Crouch, and drummer Ricky Lawson—who had all performed with Babyface—and singers Charlean Hines and Chyna. The latter had worked with Seal, Peter Gabriel, and The Who, as well as her own band. Steve Gadd would return for the second leg. Tim Carmon has been in Clapton's bands on and off ever since.

A month before the tour began, Eric announced the opening of Crossroads Centre, an addiction treatment centre on Antigua. To raise funds, Clapton auctioned one hundred of his guitars, including 'Brownie'—the guitar on which he recorded 'Layla'—at Christie's in New York. The auction raised almost $5 million. A benefit concert at Madison Square Garden on 30 June 1999 added to this, and a series of multi-artist festivals would follow.

'My Father's Eyes' (Clapton)
Released as single, February 1998. Highest chart positions: UK: 33, US Adult Contemporary: 7.

First performed at the taping for MTV's *Unplugged* on 16 January 1992. Eric to *Guitar World* in 2008:

> It's a song about Conor. I had a kind of revelation about my son. It's a very personal matter, but I never met my father, and I realized that the closest I ever came to looking into my father's eyes was when I looked into my son's eyes. So I wrote this song about that. It's a strange kind of cycle thing that occurred to me, and another thing I felt I would like to share. This was the hardest song to record on that album. 'My Father's Eyes' went through five incarnations, and I would veto it each time because at the time, it was purely from an artistic point of view that I said, 'It's too fast. It's too jolly. Or it's too sad'. Now I actually think, subconsciously, I just wasn't ready to let go, because it meant— on some level—letting go of my son.

This first version of 'My Father's Eyes' was not included on *Unplugged*, despite being recorded twice during the sessions. A central section ('are you really so far away') was eventually removed. A faster 1992 electric version includes this same mid-song bridge. By 1998, the tempo and feel have returned the *Unplugged* arrangement, but now it's more meditative, played on a shimmering electric guitar and with a rewritten central section; repeating the chorus, dropping the bridge in favour of returning to the opening hook, and adding some tasty dobro.

'My Father's Eyes' is a major song in the Clapton catalogue. It won Best Male Pop Vocal Performance at the 41st Annual Grammy Awards.

'River of Tears' (Clapton, Climie)
This is a stately 6/8 ballad, very slow, almost haunting in its deeply felt sentiment. Clapton's singing is terrific here – he had given up smoking and it shows. The strings swell and build to a spine-tingling slide guitar solo. Clapton spoke about the song to *Guitar World* in 1998:

Lyrically, it is about a specific person. My impulse for writing the song was initially very manipulative. I was always toying with the idea that when she'd hear this song, there would be a reconciliation or something. It had a purpose. Then it started getting vindictive and at some point I started feeling like the lyrics were becoming too melodramatic. I realized that the way to save it was to bring it back to talking about me, that whole thing in the song about just drifting from town to town and not really being able to fit in takes the blame off somebody else and places it on myself.

The nine-minute 2001 live version on *One More Car, One More Rider* adds a gospel twist which lifts this song from very good to phenomenal.

'Pilgrim' (Clapton, Climie)
Released as single, November 1998. Did not chart in the US or UK.

Brilliant soulful vocals *à la* Curtis Mayfield don't hide a monotonous backing track – which started as a drum backing track, as Clapton told the BBC in 1998:

We would say something like 'uh, well, um, have you heard the new Usher single?' And from there, we'd just copy the drum program, dicker with it and play along with it. That's how the song 'Pilgrim' was born. We came up with a drum program that was derived from a hit – I can't remember which one – we changed it a little and then wrote the words. We just created an atmosphere, and instantly the words were coming into my head because the mood evoked all of the circumstances that had been happening for the past few years.

Most listeners will have skipped the track or mentally switched off by the time the short, expressive guitar solo gives the song some life.

'Broken Hearted' (Clapton, Phillinganes)

A long, very slow and gentle song, with shimmering guitar and Paul Brady's tooting tin whistle. Musically sophisticated and with a great lead vocal, it's let down by a lethargic arrangement and cliched lyrics.

Clapton wrote 'Broken Hearted' in Antigua during a tropical storm. The song was first performed at the Music for Montserrat concert in London on 15 September 1997 and included with several other new songs on a short Far East tour the following month.

'One Chance' (Clapton, Climie)

Contemporary R'n'B, stately and passionate in equal measure. Pino Palladino's funky bass underpins some welcome lead guitar breaks and a very good lead vocal performance.

'Circus' (Clapton)

Released as single, June 1998. Highest chart position: UK: 39

Clapton's most recent top 40 single in his home country, the delicate 'Circus', is slick modern folk-pop-blues of the highest order. As Eric Clapton recalled in a 1998 interview with the BBC:

The last night I spent with Conor, we went to the circus. We went to see one of those huge things that they do in America where they have three rings going on at the same time. You've got clowns and tigers and everything. They don't do anything in half measures. They just pile it all in. Plus, they're trying to sell you things at the same time. I mean it was an amazing thing. After the show, we were driving back to New York and all he could remember, all he could talk about was this clown. He'd seen a clown with a knife, which I didn't see at all. Some clown was running around brandishing a knife, which was something quite frightening, but he liked it – I mean, it excited him. And so that is in the lyrics. But, and I suppose what I was doing, I was remembering, I mean paying tribute to this night with him, and also seeing him as being the circus of my life. You know – that particular part of my life has now left town.

Clapton first performed 'Circus' (then called 'Circus Left Town') for *MTV Unplugged* on 16 January 1992. This heartbreakingly sad version can be heard on the 2013 reissue of Clapton's *Unplugged* album. The 1998 version is snappier, perhaps more wistful than mournful, with a touching vocal at the bottom of Clapton's range.

'Going Down Slow' (Oden)

A cover of a St. Louis Jimmy Oden blues standard which is given a slick new arrangement and vocal melody. It's unrecognisable as the song recorded by Howlin' Wolf in 1961 (and by Clapton in 1971 and 1978).

'Fall Like Rain' (Clapton)
Eight songs in, and we have some pace in a track – 'Fall Like Rain' has hints of country bounce. Eric's brilliant vocal is drenched in reverb, however.

> Writing that song was just simply tuning back into music in my teens. I was listening to folk music, and the more I listened to that, I got deeply moved and influenced by bluegrass and Appalachian music, especially the sort of field recordings that were available. In the old days, you used to be able to go buy records on a label called Folkways. They'd have unknown people on there just playing five-string banjos, people who probably just recorded in their homes. They would just have this incredible power and sound. It was unsophisticated and crude and raw. Writing that song was tuning back into that part of my musical heritage.
> Eric Clapton, BBC interview, 1998

'Born in Time' (Dylan)
Released as single, July 1998. Did not chart in UK or US.

A straightforward cover of Bob Dylan's song, first released in 1990. This is closer to Clapton's work in the 1970s and 80s, despite the pounding drum machine. The return of Eric's dobro is always welcome, and the strings and Babyface's backing vocals suit the song well. Again, Eric's singing is excellent. The single edit removes forty-five seconds.

'Sick and Tired' (Clapton, Climie)
An overlong off-the-cuff blues with a quirky, off-kilter programmed drum pattern. Eric explained to *Guitar World* in 2011:

> The riff came first and I just thought of the Vaughan brothers. I told Simon (Climie) to program a shuffle and exaggerate the back beat so it would sound like a Texas-style groove. I began improvising silly lyrics and thought: 'Well, I might as well make it a song now.' It's a spoof, really.

Spoof or not, this is an experiment that should have stayed in the can. Sample lyrics: 'I'm gonna get me a shotgun, baby / Keep it stashed behind the bedroom door / I may have to blow your brains out, baby / Then you won't bother me no more.'

'Needs His Woman' (Clapton)
Very much in the 'Change the World' vein, 'Needs His Woman' is acoustic, gentle and smooth, probably unduly ignored three-quarters of the way through this long, uncompromising album. It's worth a revisit.

'She's Gone' (Clapton, Climie)
Finally, a faster tempo and some funky electric guitar to offer some contrast

from the introspection. One wishes for a looser feel with a real drummer, though. 'She's Gone' worked particularly well in concert in 1998 and 2001.

'You Were There' (Clapton)

A song for Clapton's long-time manager, Roger Forrester, as Eric explains at whereseric.com:

> I went around to the news agents on a Sunday morning [in August 1997] and it was on the front page that Princess Diana was dead. All this stuff started coming up like it did for everybody. For me, it was like a compilation of feelings that go back to every loss that I've ever experienced. And I had this feeling ... and I didn't want it to get pinned onto this event. I wanted to actually place it somewhere where I felt it really belonged. And so I took it to a relationship that I have been involved with myself for the last 25 years, which is with my manager. And I took this feeling and put it in this song for him.

Enjoy the musicianship, arrangement and vocal performance, but don't listen to the lyrics, which verge on saccharine.

'Inside of Me' (Clapton, Climie)

Remix released February 1998, B-side of 'My Father's Eyes'.

A modern take on Curtis Mayfield, with more drum loops and samples, and another great Clapton lead vocal; almost entirely in falsetto. A very different remix was released as the B-side of 'My Father's Eyes'.

Other Contemporary Tracks
'Theme From a Movie That Never Happened' (Clapton)

Released on the Japanese version of *Pilgrim* and also on the 'My Father's Eyes' CD single. This is a perfect acoustic guitar instrumental with delicate orchestral accompaniment. French chanteuse Françoise Hardy wrote lyrics for this piece, naming it 'Contre Vents et Marées', which translates as 'Through Thick and Thin' (or, less literally, 'Against All Odds'). This is available on Hardy's 2000 album *Clair-Obscur* and is a slightly edited version of Clapton's original piece with a vocal overdub.

'Blue Eyes Blue' (Warren)

Released as a single July 1999. Highest chart placings: UK: 94, US: 112.

'Blue Eyes Blue' was recorded at Ocean Way/Record One Studios, Los Angeles, in the summer of 1999 for the soundtrack of the romantic comedy film *Runaway Bride* starring Julia Roberts and Richard Gere. It was written by Diane Warren, the author of nine US number one singles. Warren has won the Oscar for Best Original Song on eleven occasions.

'Blue Eyes Blue' is very much in the vein of 'Change the World', mostly acoustic with a lyrical guitar solo and an excellent low register lead vocal. The recording features Greg Curtis and Jamie Muhoberac (keyboards), Tim Pierce and Darryl Crooks (guitar), Luis Conte and Mike Fasano (percussion), and the rhythm section of Nathan East and Steve Ferrone.

Clapton returned to Ocean Way for sessions for his next two albums.

'Blue Eyes Blue' is available on the 1999 compilation album *Clapton Chronicles: The Best of Eric Clapton*.

'(I) Get Lost' (Clapton)
Released as a single November 1999. Did not chart in the US or UK.

'(I) Get Lost' was originally written and recorded for the soundtrack to the 1999 film *The Story of Us*. In the film it is a beautiful, heartfelt Latin-influenced acoustic track. The soundtrack album, co-credited to Marc Shaiman, presents a further sixteen snippets of acoustic music based around '(I) Get Lost'. It's more than wonderful – like Eric Clapton is strumming and humming in your sitting room.

The single version is very different, with a busy, percussion-heavy backing track which threatens to overwhelm the song. Stick to the acoustic version.

Available on the 1999 album *Clapton Chronicles: The Best of Eric Clapton*.

Riding with the King (2000)

Personnel:
Eric Clapton and B. B. King: guitar, vocals
Doyle Bramhall II: guitar, backing vocals
Andy Fairweather Low: guitar
Joe Sample: acoustic piano, Wurlitzer piano
Tim Carmon: organ
Paul Waller: programming
Nathan East: bass
Steve Gadd: drums
Susannah and Wendy Melvoin: backing vocals
Jimmie Vaughan: guitar on 'Help the Poor'
Recorded at Ocean Way Recording, Los Angeles, and at the Town House, London.
Produced by Eric Clapton and Simon Climie. Released June 2000.
Highest chart positions: UK: 15, US: 3

An influence on every guitar player of Eric Clapton's generation, B. B. King was the real deal, despite the glitz of his live shows and a decidedly patchy recording career (*King of the Blues: 1989*, anyone?). Eric:

Over thirty years since we had first jammed together at the Café Au Go Go, I finally cut the album with B. B. King that he and I had been talking about for a long time. Working with B. B. was a dream come true, and I put together a band that I felt could rise to the occasion. I remembered the Atlantic session years ago with Aretha, where there were wall-to-wall guitar players, and thought I'd like to give that concept a try. On bass, it was Nathan East as usual, Steve Gadd on drums, Tim Carmen and Joe Sample on keyboards, and Doyle Bramhall, Andy Fairweather Low and myself on guitars.

Clapton very much took the lead in arranging the sessions, choosing the songs and booking musicians. There was a week's pre-production and a week of recording sessions. Bassist Nathan East commented to the *San Diego Tribune* in 2020:

The week before recording began, we determined what the key and tempo of each song would be. And we worked out arrangements, not really complex arrangements, to form ideas and determine if you would have a modulation in a song or not, and where. The week was more about getting comfortable in that environment and getting to know how you feel in the studio.

Eric:

We put that time aside, I got the musicians together, and it was a great experience for all of us. I don't think I can remember being in a situation that

… potent, where everyone involved was the best musician we could find on the day. We sometimes had three, maybe four, guitarists on the floor, including B.B. and myself, and the drummer and bass player and keyboards and everything, and we were sitting opposite one another, singing live. So most of the album was done first, second take – absolutely live. There was very little to do in terms of mixing or putting the record together. It was such a magical experience.

Nathan East recalls the good-natured vibe at the sessions:

The dynamic between them was almost like two guys constantly opening the door for one another. Eric would ask B.B.: 'What do you think of that?' And B.B. would say: 'If you like it, I like it.' It was a really close mutual admiration they had for each other – both giving the other guy a big, wide, musical lane to function in – extreme reverence. There was definitely a feeling of mutual respect between them. And, obviously, they each honoured the other one's ideas. It was kind of funny because they were so kind and gentle bouncing ideas off each other that it was almost laughable. One of them would say: 'Well, however you want to do this is good with me.' And the other would say: 'Well, however you want to do it is good with me.'

Riding With the King **marks Eric Clapton's first collaboration with guitarist Doyle Bramhall II. Bramhall had turned heads after two well-received solo albums and as a member of Texan blues-rock band Arc Angels. Bramhall was committed to a lengthy tour with Roger Waters but was available for the recording sessions for** *Riding With the King***. He has been a regular member of Clapton's band from 2004 to date. The presence of Joe Sample on these sessions cannot be underestimated; his piano playing is very much at the centre of the arrangements.**

Riding With the King **contains re-workings of five older B.B. King songs from the 1950s and 1960s, new arrangements of 'Key to the Highway' and 'Worried Life Blues', which Clapton had recorded in the 1970s, two songs reworked from Doyle Bramhall's most recent album, and a carefully selected cover version. King:**

My friend, Eric Clapton. He's a fabulous guy. I've always wanted to do something with him, but it's like, you don't ask friends to do things all the time – because you're friends, you know what I mean? But I always wanted to, and when I heard him tell Larry King that he would like to do something with me, man, I was on cloud nine. I told him to pick all of the tunes and if I disagreed, we'd talk about it – and we didn't. He had such a memory for bringing up old tunes, and such a great idea for getting new ones together. So I trust him completely.

Although it might be argued that *Riding With the King* plays to Clapton's middle-aged, middle-class, predominantly white audience, it is very much a payback to a major inspiration. Much of it is thrillingly authentic, and *Riding With the King* is by far the best of Clapton's three blues-based albums recorded between 1994 and 2004. It would sell over two million copies, win the Grammy for Best Traditional Blues Album in 2001, and was King's highest-ever charting album in both the US and the UK. A 20th-anniversary reissue adds two previously unreleased tracks.

Shortly after the album was recorded, Clapton was inducted into the Rock And Roll Hall Of Fame for the third time. He is the first and only triple inductee, having been previously honoured in 1992 with The Yardbirds and in 1993 with Cream.

'Riding With the King' (Hiatt)
An apposite song choice, the title track from John Hiatt's 1983 album. Clapton and King stick closely to the original arrangement, converting it to a guitar-heavy rock-blues duet, not so far in feeling and tempo from King's collaboration with U2 'When Loves Comes to Town'.

Hiatt reworked the lyrics for the King and Clapton collaboration: 'a red cape and shiny cold 45' in the original becomes 'a tuxedo and shiny 335' in this version; 335 is a reference to King's trademark Gibson guitar.

'Ten Long Years' (Taub, King)
Joe Sample's tasty piano and Doyle Bramhall's dirty slide guitar underpin a faithful reworking of a B. B. King single from 1955. Forty-five years on, King's peerless vocals have a real note of resigned maturity and regret. Clapton pulls off a terrific guitar solo, matched by B.B.'s impeccable right-hand vibrato technique.

'Key to the Highway' (Broonzy, Segar)
Memorably recorded in a single take for *Layla And Other Assorted Love Songs* in 1970, this joyous new version is gentler, sung by Clapton and King as a duet. As Clapton recalled to *Guitarist* in 2003:

When I was about 14, I saw Big Bill Broonzy on TV and that was an incredible thing. Because maybe if I'd just heard it, it might not have had the same effect. But to see footage of Broonzy playing 'Hey Hey', this was a real blues artist and I felt like I was looking into heaven. That was it for me, and then, when I went to explore his music, the song that always came back to me was an incredible version of 'Key to the Highway'. That was the one that I thought somehow would capture the whole journey of being a musician and a travelling journeyman.

B. B. King playing acoustic guitar is a rare treat.

I played some acoustic. Eric suggested we do some, uh, people call it unplugged things. I call it acoustic things. We both had acoustic guitars on some and it sounds good.

Clapton would open his concerts in 2001 with a magnificent solo acoustic version of this song.

'Marry You' (Bramhall, Melvoin, Ross)
A funky, soulful blues which first appeared on Doyle Bramhall's *Jellycream* album in 1999. Sung by Clapton and King in turn, King's distinctive guitar is like a third voice here. Clapton plays a very clean lead guitar solo.

'Three O'Clock Blues' (Fulson)
'Three O'Clock Blues' was B. B. King's first hit, one of the best-selling R'n'B singles of 1952. It was written by Lowell Fulson – Clapton recorded two of Fulson's songs, 'Reconsider Baby' and 'Sinner's Prayer' for *From the Cradle*. King and Clapton's version burns slowly: pure blues, commanding and weary. Both sing brilliantly and they trade impeccable guitar solos. This is the real deal.

'Help the Poor' (Singleton)
Released as a single, 2000. Did not chart.

A 1964 single for King as well as the last track on his legendary *Live at the Regal* recorded that same year. This re-recording does not quite match the impact of the original, despite excellent vocals from King and Clapton and backing vocals by Susannah and Wendy Melvoin, which match the 1964 arrangement. Eric's old friend (and Doyle Bramhall's former bandmate) Jimmie Vaughan adds a gritty guitar solo, as Eric explains:

One one track Jimmie Vaughan joined us, and his contribution worked so well. I kind of wished I'd asked him to play on each song.

'I Wanna Be' (Bramhall, Sexton)
A second cover from Doyle Bramhall's *Jellycream* (1999). Clapton pushes this harder than Bramhall's original, and King is a little left behind in the busy arrangement of a funky rock song, competent rather than inspirational.

'Worried Life Blues' (Hopkins, Merriweather)
'Worried Life Blues' is a blues standard previously recorded by King in 1960 (as 'Someday Baby') and 1970 (as 'Ain't Gonna Worry My Life Anymore'), and released as live versions by Clapton recorded in 1978 (*Crossroads 2: Live in the Seventies*), 1979 (*Just One Night*), 1991 (*24 Nights*), and 1992 (*Unplugged* 2013 re-issue). The King/Clapton version takes the *Unplugged* arrangement and

slows it down a touch – it's like two friends sitting on their porch at sundown picking their acoustics, with King in particularly fine form.

'Days of Old' (Taub, King)
'Days of Old' was a 1958 B-side for King. He recalled in 2000:

> We did a thing called 'Days of Old'. I can't even remember when I wrote it, but it had to be in the early fifties. It sure swings better now. As you go on you have ideas for things and you think they're good. You can't teach an old dog new tricks, but you can teach him new ways of doing the old ones.

This jumping shuffle version has overlapping exchanges of vocals and guitars, held together by Joe Sample's barrelhouse piano.

'When My Heart Beats Like a Hammer' (Taub, King)
A Top 10 R'n'B chart single for B. B. King in 1954, based on the earlier 'Million Years Blues' by Sonny Boy Williamson. This gutsy blues is primordial, powerful and immediate.

'Hold On, I'm Comin'' (Hayes, Porter)
A perfect choice: a cover of Sam and Dave's 1966 soul classic which starts like a jam session, with Clapton and King trading licks over a swampy beat. The I-bVII-IV-I chord progression pushes the chorus forward, and the arrangement is both full and dynamic. This is soulful blues at its best.

'Come Rain or Come Shine' (Arlen, Mercer)
An unexpected finale of an unusual but successful selection: a cover from the 1946 musical *St. Louis Woman*, recorded by Ray Charles, Judy Garland, Ella Fitzgerald and Frank Sinatra. King evidently needed persuading to sing this, even though it's not far from previous recordings of his such as 'Hold On (I Feel Our Love Is Changing)' from *Midnight Believer* (1978) or his 1982 cover of 'Love Me Tender'. King:

> [Eric] only picked two things that I didn't like. One of the songs that I didn't want to do was 'Come Rain or Come Shine', but he, um ... ha-ha – he's a very ... Oh, I don't know how to say it ... But he's like my girlfriend – he can persuade me to do anything he wants. So he would say to me, 'B, I listened to it, and I can hear you doin' it, so why don't you try it?' And when I did try it, it didn't sound so bad after all.

Other Contemporary Tracks
'Rollin' and Tumblin'' (Newbern)
A hardy perennial, already recorded twice by Clapton: on *Fresh Cream* in 1966, and as a spontaneous performance during the sessions for *Unplugged* in 1992.

101

The best-known version of this blues classic is Muddy Waters' Chess recording from 1950. This sounds like a warm-up or first-time run through. Eric plays dobro, B. B. picks Lucille and both sing. Released on the 2020 deluxe edition of *Riding With the King*.

'Let Me Love You' (King, Ling)

Despite the information provided at the time of release, this is not the Willie Dixon song with a similar name first recorded by Buddy Guy in 1961. It's a new version of King's own 1964 cut, 'Let Me Love You, Baby', co-credited to Saul Bihari, the owner of King's record company Kent Records, using the pseudonym Sam Ling. It's a surprise that this didn't make the original album – King's vocal is committed, and there are strings and some powerful slide guitar. Eric cuts loose with a commanding guitar solo. Released on the 2020 deluxe edition of *Riding With the King*.

Reptile (2001)

Personnel:
Eric Clapton: guitar, vocals
Doyle Bramhall II and Andy Fairweather Low: guitar
Billy Preston, Tim Carmon and Joe Sample: keyboards
Paul Carrack: keyboards on 'Reptile' and 'Second Nature'
Pino Palladino: bass on 'Reptile' and 'Second Nature'
Nathan East: bass on all other tracks
Steve Gadd: drums
Paul Waller: drum programming
Paulinho da Costa: percussion
The Impressions (Reggie Torian, Sam Gooden, Fred Cash): backing vocals
Recorded at the Town House and Olympic Studios, London; Ocean Way Recording, Los Angeles; Right Track Recording, New York City. Produced by Eric Clapton and Simon Climie.
Released March 2001.
Highest chart positions: UK: 7, US: 5

It's often forgotten that soul singers such as Ray Charles and Solomon Burke had a huge influence on Eric Clapton. Curtis Mayfield was a member of The Impressions from 1958 to 1970 and enjoyed a successful solo career. His 1965 song 'People Get Ready' is one of the great songs of the twentieth century. Clapton performed at Mayfield's memorial service at the First African Methodist Episcopal Church in Los Angeles on 22 February 2000. Mayfield had died on 26 December 1999 at 57. Clapton sang 'I've Been Trying' at the service, repeating his performance from Mayfield's induction to the Rock and Roll Hall of Fame in March 1999. He had also recorded 'You Must Believe Me' for a tribute album a few years previously and was determined to work more seriously with The Impressions who had continued to perform together. Eric:

> I wanted to make the *Reptile* album using the same concept as the B.B. album. I gathered up all the guys – basically all of the same musicians, without B. B. – and went to the same place, using the same engineer, same production team, and we set about, tried to do the same thing, into practice for my own album. It was interesting because, without B.B., it didn't really work ... We started doing songs that I had stock-piled over the past two years or so, and I thought 'Well, it feels OK, but this is much harder than I thought it would be'. I under-estimated B.B.'s presence in the whole equation. I went off to Vancouver to do some fishing. I was listening to the tapes of the album out there and thinking, 'This hasn't got any magic ... at all. It's not really working' although we appeared to have got all the right ingredients. And then, in that period, I met up with some family that I have up in Canada and we were talking about the fact that my uncle had passed away, earlier in the year. Suddenly, another element came in – which was that I became inspired by the passing of my uncle, who was a very big influence in my

life. Suddenly, I got re-motivated and I went back to the studio. Then, almost accidentally, The Impressions came in, Billy Preston came in – and what was like a dead duck before, something which really wasn't happening suddenly exploded, and, in the following two weeks, we basically made my new album. I had also been a lifelong fan of Curtis Mayfield and had the honour of being invited to sing with The Impressions at his memorial service in LA. I asked if they would come and sing on the album and was over the moon when they said yes, too.

Reptile was recorded at the Town House in London, with further sessions in Los Angeles and New York. The Impressions add their distinctive backing vocals to eleven of the fourteen songs.

Whilst utterly professional and with many moments of intimacy and sublimity (as well as a couple of out-and-out classics), *Reptile*, like *Pilgrim*, is overlong and uneven. As *Rolling Stone* commented at the time:

> Over the course of fourteen tracks, Clapton blends virtually every style he's worked in during the past thirty-five years. Whether it will strike your ears as something-for-everyone generosity or a patchy jumble, probably depends on how much of a purist you are.

The four-leg, one-hundred-date *Reptile* tour employed a smaller band: Andy Fairweather Low, Nathan East, Steve Gadd, and new-comer David Sancious, an early member of the E Street Band and long-time touring musician with Stanley Clarke, Sting, Peter Gabriel, Zucchero and others. The Impressions performed on many dates on the tour. Billy Preston was added to the band for the North American concerts, including the recording of the live album *One More Car, One More Rider*. Doyle Bramhall II was the support act for the US dates.

'Reptile' (Clapton)
A smooth jazz samba, drawing a direct line from 'Peaches and Diesel' and 'Signe' through Eric's work with Legends in 1997. The track would win the award for Best Pop Instrumental Performance at the 44th Annual Grammys. On the live version released on *One More Car, One More Rider*, Eric and his top-notch band make very difficult music look effortless and sound great.

'Got You on My Mind' (Thomas, Briggs)
An obscure Big Joe Turner song from 1959, also covered by Jerry Lee Lewis and Brook Benton. 'Got You on My Mind' is ideally suited to this up-beat R'n'B arrangement. The Impressions add their distinctive 'doo-wah' backing vocals. This song worked particularly well in Eric's acoustic sets in 2001.

'Travelin' Light' (Cale)
A track from J. J. Cale's fourth studio album *Troubadour*, released in 1976. His original version of 'Cocaine' was on the same album. As with previous Cale

covers, Clapton takes the Cale formula and applies a tougher arrangement, overlaid with gritty blues guitar licks. The Impressions' backing vocals give a new twist to an old formula.

'Believe in Life' (Clapton)
An original composition in the 'Signe' mould, cited by Eric Clapton in *Uncut* (2015) as his best song.

> I wrote it about my wife. I like the fact that it's kind of low-key, a little in-the-background thing, but I'm proud of that song, as much as anything of mine that's more popular or well-known.

It's a heartfelt, minor chord love song with some jazzy changes and B. B. King-style electric guitar interjections. The final section is lifted by The Impressions' gospel-influenced backing vocals.

'Come Back Baby' (Charles)
A return to Ray Charles, 'Come Back Baby' is similar to Clapton's earlier version of 'Hard Times'. Clapton's arrangement is note-for-note the same as Charles' 1954 recording, with added blues guitar and backing vocals. Clapton sings and plays well, and Billy Preston plays up a storm, but the end result is curiously sterile.

'Broken Down' (Climie, Morgan)
A lightweight mid-paced soul ballad saved by a great chorus, with Eric and The Impressions on good form.

'Find Myself' (Clapton)
More jazz/R'n'B changes, slow and introspective, but ultimately uplifting.

'I Ain't Gonna Stand for It' (Wonder)
Released as a single, April 2001. Did not chart in the UK or US.

Clapton's marvellous take on Stevie Wonder's 'I Ain't Gonna Stand for It' has an appealingly commercial and soulful groove that suits Clapton like an old denim jacket. Eric to Mike Hrano in 2001:

> It's a song where [Wonder is] kind of sending up country music, and because he's singing like a white guy in the verses, I find that quite easy to imitate!

Wonder's original is on *Hotter Than July* (1982) and was a big hit single. Clapton's version pays tribute and adds some blues seasoning. A triumph.

'I Want a Little Girl' (Mencher, Moll)
A fabulous jazzy slow blues first released by McKinney's Cotton Pickers in 1930.

The vocals here from Clapton and The Impressions are superlative. This is every inch as good as 'Hard Times' from *Journeyman*.

'Second Nature' (Clapton, Climie, Morgan)
A new song that sounds old, with a gutsy acoustic arrangement and Clapton singing in his lowest range. Slide guitar and Hammond organ colour the chorus, and again The Impressions lift the song with their peerless backing vocals.

'Don't Let Me Be Lonely Tonight' (Taylor)
A romantic ballad, written by James Taylor and released on *One Man Dog* in 1972. Clapton's source for this version is a soulful 6/8 re-arrangement by The Isley Brothers from their *3+3* album (1973). Clapton is always considered a world-class guitarist, quite rightly, but his singing had improved significantly since he gave up smoking. On this song, his vocal performance is nothing short of outstanding, with startling range, impeccable phrasing and genuine passion. He is backed by The Impressions and a smooth string section. What a song!

'Modern Girl' (Clapton)
A gentle love song, clear in its message but perhaps needing a stronger lyric. Like many of Clapton's own songs post-*Unplugged*, this is performed on nylon-strung acoustic guitar and employs many augmented and suspended chords with a slight Latin hint to the rhythm. Again, The Impressions' contribution adds significantly to the arrangement.

A significantly different version circulates on bootleg, claiming to be an outtake from *Pilgrim*. This might well be genuine.

'Superman Inside' (Clapton, Bramhall, Melvoin)
Co-written with husband-and-wife team Doyle Bramhall II and Susannah Melvoin, 'Superman Outside' is about finding confidence and peace of mind as you face challenges and is therefore relatable to every listener. It's closer to Clapton's work with Jerry Lynn Williams than his more recent work, and therefore feels a little out of place here.

'Son and Sylvia' (Clapton)
A gentle, elegant, sad, swooning guitar instrumental. It's dedicated to his late uncle, Adrian. Eric:

[My uncle] was a very, very pivotal person in my early learning days. What happened with his passing was that I was reintroduced to that fact. When he died, I hadn't seen him for quite a long time – we'd kind of grown apart. A lot of that was to do with my leaving home and then...never really going back.

Other Contemporary Tracks
'Losing Hand' (Stone)
A strong, soulful 6/8 blues released on the CD single of 'Ain't Gonna Stand for It' and as Japanese bonus track. Perhaps another Ray Charles cover was one too many for the album, but this is an excellent performance that deserves wider recognition.

'Johnny Guitar' (Young, Lee)
A seven-minute instrumental version of a Peggy Lee song, played in 5/4 time, released on the CD single of 'Ain't Gonna Stand for It'. There's obviously no place on a commercial album for a self-indulgent piece such as this, but that doesn't stop it being tremendous.

'Just Walkin' in the Rain' (Riley, Bragg)
A cover of The Prisonaires' song from 1952, recorded with The Impressions and released in 2001 on the various artists' tribute album *Good Rockin' Tonight: The Legacy of Sun Records*. Doo-wop meets slide guitar. Wonderful.

'I'm a Changed Man (Finally Got Myself Together)' (Townsend)
A song by The Impressions, written and produced by Ed Townsend – co-writer of 'Let's Get It On' – and first released 1974 on the album of the same name. This was one of five songs that The Impressions sang on the *Reptile* tour.

'It's All Right' (Mayfield)
A Curtis Mayfield song first released by The Impressions in 1963 and performed by Clapton with The Impressions on the *Reptile* tour.

'Will It Go Round in Circles?' (Preston, Fisher)
Billy Preston's show-stopping spotlight number on the 2001 US tour, first released by him in 1972. Available on the DVD version of *One More Car, One More Rider*.

'Over the Rainbow' (Arlen, Harburg)
Eric's encore on his 2001 tour; a brilliantly and delicately performed rendition of one of the greatest songs of the twentieth century. Available on *One More Car, One More Rider*.

'What Would I Do Without You' (Charles)
Clapton sang this 1956 track by his hero Ray Charles on *Small World Big Band* (2001), the first of a series of collaboration albums by Jools Holland, his R'n'B Orchestra, and many A-list guests. The singing is astonishing, the arrangement uplifting, and the playing simply out of this world.

Me and Mr. Johnson / Sessions for Robert J (2004)

Personnel:
Eric Clapton: guitar, slide guitar, vocals
Andy Fairweather Low: guitar
Doyle Bramhall II: guitar, slide guitar
Billy Preston: acoustic piano, Hammond organ
Nathan East: bass
Pino Palladino: bass on 'Traveling Riverside Blues'
Steve Gadd: drums
Jim Keltner: drums on 'Traveling Riverside Blues'
Jerry Portnoy: harmonica
Me and Mr Johnson recorded in 2004 at the Town House, London. Produced by
Eric Clapton and Simon Climie. Released March 2004.
Highest chart positions: UK:10, US: 6
Sessions for Robert J recorded March 2004 at Hook End Manor; June 2004 at
Studios Las Colinas, Irving; June 2004 at 508 Park Avenue, Dallas; and August 2004
at Hotel Casa Del Mar, Santa Monica. Released December 2004.
Highest chart positions: US: 171, UK: did not chart

Eric Clapton married Melia McEnery on 3 January 2002 and spent most of 2002
and 2003 off the road with his new wife and their young daughters.

He appeared at two major concert events in 2002. The Party at the Palace,
on 3 June 2002, finally moved rock music from 'current' to 'retro'. Eric added
guitar to Brian Wilson's and Paul McCartney's sets and, perhaps inevitably, sang
'Layla'.

More positively, the Concert for George took place at the Royal Albert Hall
on 29 November 2002. Eric was musical director of this amazing tribute to
his friend George Harrison, who had died exactly one year before. Eric added
acoustic guitar to the Ravi Shankar piece 'Arpan' and provided his regular band
(Andy Fairweather Low, Chris Stainton, Henry Spinetti and Dave Bronze) for
a set of George's best-known songs. He was joined for one or more songs by
Jim Capaldi, Albert Lee, Ray Cooper, Gary Brooker, Dhani Harrison and Jim
Keltner, as well as some high-profile guests: Paul McCartney, Ringo Starr, Tom
Petty and the Heartbreakers, Billy Preston, Jeff Lynne, Jools Holland, Sam
Brown and Joe Brown. Eric played on every song, and sings on 'If I Needed
Someone', 'Beware of Darkness', 'Isn't It a Pity' (duet with Billy Preston),
'Something' (duet with Paul McCartney), 'While My Guitar Gently Weeps' and
'Wah-Wah'. The CD and DVD of this fabulous show were released in November
2003.

Early the following year, Clapton commenced recording his fifteenth solo
album at The Town House with producer Simon Climie and his current band,
intending to record a batch of new songs to reflect on his new wife and family.
Eric:

It is not an easy thing to do, writing songs about happiness, but I wanted to bear witness to how radically my life had changed. [The songs] just weren't coming, but I knew there was no sense in trying to force it. They would come when the time was right. We did have studio time booked, however, and when the day arrived to begin recording, it was clear that we didn't have enough material to work with. So I came up with the idea that whenever there was a lull, we would play a Robert Johnson song to relieve the tension and just have some fun. Within two weeks, we had a complete Robert Johnson tribute album without ever having had any intention to do anything of the kind. It just grew out of necessity, from nothing.

Robert Johnson was born in Hazlehurst, Mississippi, possibly on 8 May 1911. After an eventful childhood, he became friendly with local blues musician Son House. It's here where the legend says that Robert Johnson made a Faustian pact with the devil: in exchange for his soul, Johnson was taught how to play the blues. Make of this what you will. What is certain is that he took up as an itinerant musician after 1932 and recorded twenty-nine songs in total during sessions in San Antonio between 23-27 November 1936 and in Dallas on 19 and 20 June 1937. Most of these were released on 78rpm singles between 1937 and 1939. Johnson died of a burst ulcer on 16 August 1938, at the age of 27, near Greenwood, Mississippi, brought on by poisoning, evidently by a jealous husband.

The album *King of the Delta Blues Singers*, released in 1961, consists of sixteen of Johnson's recordings.

King of the Delta Blues Singers was a landmark for several important reasons: It made Robert's music available to a new generation and audience–mostly young whites who were involved in the folk music revival. It boldly proclaimed Robert to be the king of the Delta blues singers; there was no one better. As the first major-label reissue of any of the guitar-oriented country blues artists from the 1920s or 1930s, there was no other music to compare it to – Robert Johnson was it, the new generation's first experience in hearing the Delta blues. And it strongly influenced such future trendsetters as a young Bob Dylan, Eric Clapton, and Keith Richards. They became Robert Johnson proselytizers.

Bruce Conforth and Gayle Dean Wardlow, *Up Jumped the Devil: The Real Life of Robert Johnson* (2019)

For Eric Clapton, this was the motherlode:

Robert Johnson was so intense. It was difficult for me to take in when I first heard *King of The Delta Blues Singers*. I thought it was really non-musical, very raw. Then I went back to it later and got into it. [On] first hearing it was just too much anguish to take on. I knew from the day I heard the album, maybe the second or third time, which was when I was sixteen or seventeen, that I'd come to the end of the road, really. In a very short amount of time, I'd gone from the Kalin Twins, through Buddy Holly, Elvis, Carl Perkins, Eddie Cochran, into Chuck Berry, Bo Diddley, Muddy Waters, Elmore James, Big Bill Broonzy, and back finally to Robert Johnson – and that's where the road ended. There was no deeper you could dig.

Eric Clapton's first recorded lead vocal was Johnson's 'Rambling on My Mind', from the Bluesbreakers' *Beano* album (1965). Cream recorded 'Four Until Late' in 1966, and 'Crossroads' in 1968 – a rock classic. Clapton laid down other Johnson songs in 1974 ('Steady Rollin' Man', *461 Ocean Boulevard*), 1992 ('Walking Blues' and 'Malted Milk', *Unplugged*) and 1994 ('32-20 Blues', single B-side). *Me and Mr Johnson* contains a new version of '32-20 Blues', as well as thirteen other songs recorded by Clapton's hero. It stands as a fine tribute to Robert Johnson, more personal and intimate than *From the Cradle*. Eric:

He's the most important influence I've had in my life and always will be, I think.

We should note here that Clapton's contemporary, Peter Green, had recorded almost the entire Robert Johnson catalogue on *The Robert Johnson Songbook* (1997) and *Hot Foot Powder* (2000). Todd Rundgren released an album of twelve Robert Johnson songs in 2011.

Me and Mr Johnson was released in March 2004. Three months later, Clapton organised and performed at the first Crossroads Guitar Festival in Dallas, Texas. This three-day event presented the cream of the world's guitarists in a benefit event for the Crossroads Centre in Antigua. A two-disc DVD presents highlights. A second guitar auction in June 2004 raised $6 million for the foundation and included the sale of 'Blackie,' Eric's legendary Fender Stratocaster, and the cherry red Gibson ES-335, known as 'The Cream Guitar'. A third guitar auction in March 2011 raised an additional $1.75 million. Eric also presented four further Crossroads Guitar Festivals in 2007, 2010, 2013 and 2019. Proceeds from sales of CDs and DVDs, including two multi-disc collections, continue to benefit the Crossroads Centre Foundation. Those with very deep pockets can treat themselves to the eye-wateringly expensive *Six-String Stories,* Clapton's own descriptions of his guitar collection.

From 2004 onwards, Clapton would generally select his live bands from a small pool of familiar names: Andy Fairweather Low or Doyle Bramhall II on guitar; Chris Stainton, Tim Carmon, Walt Richmond or Paul Carrack on keyboards; Nathan East or Willie Weeks on bass; Steve Gadd, Steve Jordan or Sonny Emory on drums, and Sharon White with Michelle John, Sharlotte Gibson or Katie Kissoon on backing vocals. Bassists Pino Palladino and Dave Bronze and drummers Ian Thomas, Abe Laboriel Jr and Henry Spinetti would also perform in Clapton's line-ups in the 2010s and 2020s.

'When You Got a Good Friend' (Johnson)

The album opens with a straight mid-tempo shuffling blues song with a very live feel, not so far from *Journeyman*'s 'Before You Accuse Me'. From track one, *Me and Mr Johnson* has a much more relaxed feel than *From the Cradle*. Eric isn't baring his psyche or trying too hard: he's not being reverential, even though he is playing tribute. The results are wonderful.

'Little Queen of Spades' (Johnson)

A classy slow blues with a rich sound, including swirling Hammond organ, parping harmonica and three guitars, meshing perfectly. Eric sings brilliantly. The version from *Live in San Diego* recorded on the 2007 Derek & Doyle Tour stretches to an entirely satisfying seventeen minutes.

'They're Red Hot' (Johnson)

A perfect ragtime blues, with sparkling dobro, brushed drums, tinkling piano (Billy Preston earning his session fee), tooting harmonica, and another great lead vocal from Eric.

'Me and the Devil Blues' (Johnson)

This rather polite version of 'Me and the Devil Blues' lacks the creeping menace of Robert Johnson's original – that performance seems dredged up from the very doors of hell. But the band are tight and slick, and Jerry Portnoy's harmonica drives the arrangement to great effect. There's an astounding alternative version on the *Sessions for Robert J* film, which is just Eric and Doyle Bramhall on acoustic guitar and dobro–in the same building in Dallas as Robert Johnson's original recording session in June 1937.

'Traveling Riverside Blues' (Johnson)

Throughout the Delta region and beyond, Robert Johnson's rambling had left a trail of drunken men and broken-hearted women. Whether he was playing a juke like O'Malley's, a picnic, or a party, Robert was always looking for a woman to satisfy his needs, financially or sexually. His songs were often a tool to seduce some woman he took a fancy to, and the human remnants he left behind were well known to locals. He even bragged about his conquests in one of his songs, 'Traveling Riverside Blues': 'I got womens in Vicksburg, clean on into Tennessee / But my Friars Point rider, now, hops all over me.'
Bruce Conforth and Gayle Dean Wardlow, *Up Jumped the Devil: The Real Life of Robert Johnson* (2019)

'Travelling Riverside Blues' is a close cousin of 'Rollin' and Tumblin', first recorded in 1929 and familiar to Eric Clapton through Muddy Waters' 1950 recording. It was recorded by Cream on their debut album. Led Zeppelin's lively 1969 version of 'Travelling Riverside Blues', recorded for the BBC, is available on the re-release of their rarities album *Coda*. Eric's version is slow, stomping and dirty.

'Last Fair Deal Gone Down' (Johnson)
Astounding electric jump blues, brilliantly performed and mixed to give a real punch. There are no solos here, so the focus is purely on the band's tight performance and Eric's forceful lead vocal.

'Stop Breakin' Down Blues' (Johnson)
Piano and drums keep a strict beat, almost a march, allowing slide guitars and harmonica to float above. It's less dense than The Rolling Stones' version from *Exile on Main Street* (1972), and positively polite in comparison to The White Stripes' 1999 adaptation. There's a tad more grit in the *Sessions for Robert J* version.

'Milkcow's Calf Blues' (Johnson)
This starts as just piano and slide guitar... and then the rhythm section crashes in to add to a rolling arrangement. The alternative version on *Sessions for Robert J* has a warmer sound and a great live feel.

'Kind Hearted Woman Blues' (Johnson)
Played in Eric's live set as early as 1978 – there's a live version on *Crossroads 2: Live in the Seventies* (1996) – 'Kind Hearted Woman Blues' was the first song laid down at Robert Johnson's earliest recording session in San Antonio on 23 November 1936.

> Robert wanted to make hit records, and he borrowed 'Kind Hearted Woman Blues' from a number of sources that were already hits for other bluesmen. It was both musically and lyrically aligned with Leroy Carr's 'Mean Mistreater Mama' and Bumble Bee Slim's 'Cruel Hearted Woman Blues'. But Robert's genius was beyond just knowing good songs to copy: he rewrote them, changed the tempo, synced his guitar more closely with his vocal than those who preceded him, added a guitar riff, and literally remade the piece. Although inspired by the original, the new song was really all his.
> Bruce Conforth and Gayle Dean Wardlow, *Up Jumped the Devil: The Real Life of Robert Johnson* (2019)

Clapton nails this dark, enigmatic version – there is a superb lead vocal with a spine-tingling falsetto section, expressive guitar playing, and a tight band performance. The live-in-the-studio take on *Sessions for Robert J* is equally good, perhaps better.

Clapton chose Robert Johnson's original 'Kind Hearted Woman Blues' for a compilation cover CD to coincide with an interview with *Uncut* in May 2004.

'Come On in My Kitchen' (Johnson)

'Come On in My Kitchen' dates from 23 November 1936 and was the third track, side one, of *King of the Delta Blues Singers*. It's one of Robert Johnson's best (and best known) songs. The melody was adapted from the Mississippi Sheiks' 1930 hit 'Sitting on Top of the World', later memorably covered by Howling Wolf in 1957, and by Cream in 1968. Eric started playing the song as a solo acoustic piece on his *From the Cradle* tour and gives this arrangement a gospel/blues twist with lots of snarling dobro.

'If I Had Possession Over Judgement Day' (Johnson)

A 1936 adaptation of an even earlier song, 'Rollin' and Tumblin', recorded by Clapton with Cream in 1966 and with B. B. King in 2000. They are, in effect, the same song – even some of the verse lyrics are identical. Because of this, it is perhaps the least inspiring song on this album. The *Sessions* version has more life with plenty of slide guitar.

'Love in Vain' (Johnson)

'Love in Vain' is based upon a melody used by the blues singer Leroy Carr from his 1935 release 'When the Sun Goes Down', rearranged for guitar, and with new lyrics borrowed in part from 'The Flying Crow' by Black Ivory King, also from 1935, specifically the powerful image of a train leaving 'with two lights on behind'.

The Rolling Stones famously recorded 'Love in Vain' for their 1969 album *Let It Bleed*. Even better, track down their acoustic version on *Stripped*, recorded in Tokyo in 1995. Clapton takes the song at a faster clip, with full band. The solo acoustic version on the *Sessions for Robert J* DVD is perhaps closer to the heart of this classic blues song.

'32-20 Blues' (Johnson)

Proof that the blues doesn't have to be slow and mournful, '32-20 Blues' is a fast swing with a terrific piano solo by Billy Preston. Bob Dylan's chirpy solo acoustic version is also worth hearing.

'Hell Hound on My Trail' (Johnson)

['Hell Hound on My Trail'] is so different from his other compositions that it is often singled out as Robert's masterpiece, his most intense performance. The melody was borrowed from Skip James's 1931 Paramount recording 'Devil Got My Woman', but Robert seemed entranced, in a fearful, unexplainable mindset. Either he was suffering from deep lingering fears and trauma from the tragedies in his life, or he was a master at projecting himself into a performance and selling a song.
Bruce Conforth and Gayle Dean Wardlow, *Up Jumped the Devil: The Real Life of Robert Johnson* (2019)

Eric's vocals are strong, and his guitar is loud and distorted. The odd time signature keeps drummer Steve Gadd on his toes, but this version fails to match the intense melancholy of Robert Johnson's original. The two guitar version on the *Sessions from Robert J* film is something else entirely – breathtaking.

Other Contemporary Tracks
The companion album *Sessions for Robert J* adds a DVD of sixteen live-in-the-studio performances from four sessions throughout 2004. An accompanying CD contains eleven of these, including four songs not included on *Me and Mr Johnson*.

'Sweet Home Chicago' (Johnson)
A blues standard, played by everyone. As with many of Robert Johnson's songs, and the blues and folk traditions in general, some lyrics and melodies are borrowed from other tunes. In this case, 'Sweet Home Chicago' is very obviously based on Kokomo Arnold's 'Old Original Kokomo Blues', recorded in Chicago in September 1934. This is the kind of song Eric Clapton can sing in his sleep. Of course, his superb band provide a taut arrangement, but there's nothing here that we've not heard many times before.

This was part of Eric's blues-only set at the Royal Albert Hall in February-March 1993.

'Terraplane Blues' (Johnson)
Robert Johnson's biggest seller on 78, Clapton plays a pure country blues arrangement, just one voice and two guitars. First performed live during the blues-only set of 1993.

'From Four Until Late' (Johnson)
Recorded by Cream in 1966, and performed in a more subtle acoustic arrangement in 1993-1994. This take is simple and effective; like 'Terraplane Blues', it's just acoustic guitar, dobro and vocals.

'Ramblin' on My Mind' (Johnson)
Recorded several times over the years, firstly with John Mayall's Bluesbreakers in 1966 – Clapton's first recorded lead vocal performance. Live versions from July 1974, December 1974, December 1979, and February 2008 appear on *Crossroads 2: Live in the Seventies* (1996), *EC Was Here* (1975), *Just One Night* (1980) and *Live from Madison Square Garden* (2009). This *Sessions for Robert J* take is closest to the Robert Johnson original of all of the songs recorded for this project. It's Eric and his dobro, nothing more. Thrilling.

'Stones in My Passway' (Johnson)
A solo acoustic take recorded at the same Santa Monica session as 'Rambling

on My Mind' and 'Love in Vain' for *Sessions For Robert J*. It's on the DVD, but not on the CD. It would be recorded more formally for *I Still Do*.

Back Home (2005)

Personnel:
Eric Clapton: lead vocals, guitar
Doyle Bramhall II, Andy Fairweather Low, Vince Gill and John Mayer: guitar
Robert Randolph: pedal steel guitar
Simon Climie: keyboards, programming
Toby Baker, Billy Preston, Chris Stainton and Steve Winwood: keyboards
Nathan East, Paul Fakhourie and Pino Palladino: bass
Steve Gadd and Abe Laboriel Jr: drums
Nicky Shaw: programming, percussion
Kick Horns: brass
Gavyn Wright, Isobel Griffiths and Nick Ingman: strings
Michelle John, Sharon White and Lawrence Johnson: backing vocals
Recorded 2004–2005 at The Town House, London; Olympic Studios, London, and
Los Angeles. Produced by Eric Clapton and Simon Climie. Released August 2005.
Highest chart positions: UK: 19, US: 13

Back Home: nine new tasteful and slickly produced originals, and three
cover versions. *Entertainment Weekly*'s harsh review – '[An] overblown and
underwhelming batch of MOR gruel' – entirely misses the point. Clapton had
worked out the need to return to the nostalgia of Cream in a series of incendiary
concerts in May 2005 and was now happy to be a doting father and husband.
Back Home reflects this new domesticity. What's notable here is that since giving
up smoking, Eric's voice had matured – he sings brilliantly throughout.

A special edition format of this album features a DVD with the whole album
in surround sound, an interview with Clapton, and snippets of five selections
from the album with Eric playing along.

'So Tired' (Clapton, Climie)
The jaunty arrangement of 'So Tired' introduces a new phase in Clapton's life
and songwriting: domestic bliss. We can forgive the trite lyrics ('Sometime I
think I'll just go on to bed / I must have better things to do / When it's time to
get my good night kiss / My dreams have all come true') in exchange for the
tasty dobro which underpins the song.

'Say What You Will' (Clapton, Climie)
A gentle reggae, first released in Japan in March 2005 on the album *Love the
Earth*. It's pleasant, but forgettable.

'I'm Going Left' (Wonder, Wright)
The first of the album's highlights, 'I'm Going Left', is a tribute to Syreeta
Wright, Stevie Wonder's ex-wife and a significant artist in her own right. She
had died in July 2004. 'I'm Going Left' is the opening track on 1974's *Stevie
Wonder Presents: Syreeta*. The song and arrangement suit Clapton perfectly,

and he sings very well indeed. An album of Eric's pop-soul songs would be very good indeed.

'Love Don't Love Nobody' (Jefferson, Simmons)
An amazing, soulful cover of a 1974 track by the Detroit Spinners, which easily matches the emotional intensity of the original. Eric Clapton is a great guitarist, but here's proof that with the right material, he's a world-class singer, too. Here his performance is simply outstanding. The production is beautiful too.

'Revolution' (Clapton, Climie)
Anthony DeCurtis, *Rolling Stone*, September 2005:

> On 'Revolution', a sinuous reggae shuffle, Clapton and his deft band burn off *Back Home*'s polish and heat the track to a seductive simmer.

This is a slight song with less-than-brilliant lyrics, saved by a classy production with backing vocals, horns and percussion.

'Love Comes to Everyone' (Harrison)
Perhaps not an obvious choice to pay homage to his old friend George – the original, with Eric on lead guitar, was on Harrison's 1979 self-titled solo album. The song was also performed a few times on Harrison's 1991 tour with Clapton. The slide guitar is pure Harrison, and the vocal is full of warmth. Steve Winwood recreates his original keyboard part as well.

'Lost and Found' (Bramhall, Jeremy)
A gritty, blues-based number with some fluid guitar playing and a dynamic chorus. It was part of Eric's live set in 2006, where the intentionally unexpected cut-off at the end of the song was replicated. From a Clapton interview with the *San Diego Union Tribune*:

> Q: The song 'Lost and Found' has a very abrupt ending, in the middle of your solo, and I wonder if that was deliberate?
> Clapton: Yeah, it was an homage to D'Angelo. He knows I'm a fan of his. It was from his *Voodoo* album, a song that was very Prince-like, and he ended it the same way.

'Piece of My Heart' (Bramhall, Melvoin, Elizondo)
A slinky, soulful, mid-paced ballad – 'Change the World' with electric guitars and horns.

'One Day' (Gill, Darnall)
A bland verse with an uplifting chorus, a horn break, and two surprise full-on guitar solos which end the song on a high. The song was co-written by country

singer Vince Gill and lyricist Beverley Darnall, who writes on her website bevdm.com:

> I wrote this lyric many years ago, and I gave it to Vince Gill because he said he liked it. It was many more years before he wrote some music to go with it, and even more years before I asked my buddy Bobby Blazier to produce the demo of the song. I told him to think in the style of Eric Clapton. The rest of the story is another version of 'it's all in who you know', and it turns out I have some good friends.

'One Track Mind' (Clapton, Climie)
A slight funky groove with some welcome virtuosic dobro, and a soul-tinged chorus with backing singers and horns.

'Run Home to Me' (Clapton, Climie)
The waltz time and languid tempo immediately recall 'Beautiful Thing' from 1976's *No Reason to Cry*. Impeccable musical backing cannot hide another schmaltzy lyric, and although the sincerity cannot be doubted, the end result is lifeless. The song was performed live just once, in Glasgow on 8 May 2006.

'Back Home' (Clapton)
The final cut, the title song, is the album's only solo composition. It's based around a simple acoustic guitar figure and has a subtle horn line under the chorus. 'Back Home' provides a gentle end to a professional, slick, but generally low-key album, with two classic tracks and a handful of enjoyable songs.

Other Contemporary Tracks
'Silver Rain' (Miller, Clapton, Kibble, Withers)
Jazz-kissed contemporary R'n'B with a slight reggae lilt, from Marcus Miller's 2005 album *Silver Rain*. Clapton sings with conviction, the arrangement is impeccable, and the guitar solo sharp and short. On this evidence, one wishes that Clapton and Miller had worked together more often.

The Road to Escondido (2006)

Personnel:

J. J. Cale: guitars, keyboards, vocals

Eric Clapton: guitars, vocals

Derek Trucks, John Mayer, Albert Lee and Doyle Bramhall II: guitar

Christine Lakeland: acoustic guitar, backing vocals

Nathan East, Gary Gilmore, Willie Weeks and Pino Palladino: bass

Jim Karstein, James Cruce, Steve Jordan and Abe Laboriel Jr: drums

Simon Climie: percussion, programming

David Teegarden: percussion

Billy Preston and Walt Richmond: keyboards

Taj Mahal: harmonica

Dennis Caplinger: fiddle

Bruce Fowler, Marty Grebb, Steve Madaio and Jerry Peterson: horns

Recorded August 2005 in Los Angeles. Produced by J. J. Cale, Eric Clapton and Simon Climie. Released November 2006.

Highest chart positions: UK: 50, US: 23

The *Road to Escondido* pairs Eric Clapton with his friend and influence J. J. Cale. Clapton's 1970s versions of Cale's 'After Midnight' and 'Cocaine' are two of his most popular recordings. Whereas with B. B. King's involvement in *Riding With the King* Clapton is repaying a huge debt to a master guitarist and major post-war recording artist, J. J. Cale's fame post-dates Clapton's – in fact, Cale's success was initiated by Clapton's recording of 'After Midnight'. *The Road to Escondido*, therefore, seems misbalanced: eleven Cale songs that stick to a long-term formula, two Clapton originals, and one cover. How much you enjoy this album will depend on whether you're as big a J. J. Cale fan as his guitar-toting pal and sponsor.

This collaboration album with J. J. Cale pretty much confirms why he never became as huge as his disciples: he has very little presence. *The Road to Escondido* never picks up steam, instead stalling somewhere between goodwill effort and vanity project.
Ultimateclassicrock.com

The album is loose and relaxed, just like you'd expect. But it's not adventurous. Cale used to sing a bit behind the beat, and that's what made him different – in search of phrasing. Now he's singing right on the beat. It takes away the edge. It's boring. *The Road to Escondido* feels like a fishing trip of two old fly fishermen. They are too old to really fly fish: they just stand at the side of the water, murmuring, fiddling, and fooling around, while the water flows wildly past.
Philip D Huff, *The Twisted Ear*, 2006

119

There are an impressive number of guest performers on *The Road to Escondido*. Derek Trucks is a guitar prodigy who joined the Allman Brothers Band in 1999, aged twenty. He is the nephew of Allman Brothers' drummer Butch Trucks and would tour in Clapton's band in the years to come. Likewise, John Mayer's career was on the rise and he had appeared at the 2004 Crossroads Festival. Blues legend Taj Mahal adds harmonica, and Clapton's former, current or future band members Albert Lee, Doyle Bramhall II, Nathan East, Willie Weeks, Steve Jordan, Abe Laboriel Jr, Billy Preston and Walt Richmond also appear along with members of Cale's band.

The Road to Escondido won the award for Best Contemporary Blues Album at the 50th Annual Grammy Awards in 2007. Later that year, Clapton's compelling autobiography was published to generally positive reviews.

'Danger' (Cale)
'Danger' sets out the stall for *The Road to Escondido*: a mid-paced three-chord shuffle with thrumming Hammond organ, a languid rhythm section, joint vocals and guitar solos from Clapton and Cale.

'Heads in Georgia' (Cale)
A sleepy arrangement, relaxed and casual. It's typical of Cale's solo work, which tends to set a mood rather than worrying about dynamics.

'Missing Person' (Cale)
Crunchy lead guitar and jaunty piano colour this pleasing, sturdy song which has a perfect Derek Trucks slide guitar solo.

'When This War Is Over' (Cale)
A rewrite of 'Call Me the Breeze', 'When This War Is Over' is a bluesy shuffle which could have come from *461 Ocean Boulevard* or *Slowhand*.

'Sporting Life Blues' (McGhee)
A Brownie McGhee song first recorded in 1946. It's a straight blues which allows Clapton to use his newly rich vocals and deliver a gorgeous solo. Taj Mahal honks some harmonica.

'Dead End Road' (Cale)
'Dead End Blues' is a rollocking country tune with dancing fiddle courtesy of virtuoso bluegrass multi-instrumentalist Dennis Caplinger. Albert Lee lifts the song with a quite tasty guitar solo.

'It's Easy' (Cale)
A languid song that cranks up slowly and rolls past without really making much of a mark – as long as you don't listen to the words. Sample lyrics: 'If you wanna think she's ugly and always depressed / She can go out and buy

herself a new dress / It's easy, easy for her / Solves all of her problems, that's for sure.' Yikes.

'Hard to Thrill' (Clapton, Mayer)
'Hard to Thrill' is the undoubted highlight of the album, with a sublime Clapton vocal, thrumming organ over smart chord changes, and effortlessly melodic guitar and piano solos. Cale is restricted to backup vocals but offers a fine guitar solo of his own.

'Anyway the Wind Blows' (Cale)
Originally re-recorded for Cale's third album *Okie* (1976). This is a carbon copy with better production.

'Three Little Girls' (Clapton)
A beautiful and touching acoustic tribute to Eric's young family. 'Lord, you put me to the test / Led me through the wilderness / Then you showed me a brighter day / With three little girls.' Seemingly recorded without Cale's direct musical involvement, 'Three Little Girls' sounds out of place on *The Road to Escondido*: an exercise in careful, compact melodic songwriting amongst J. J. Cale's more one-note contributions.

'Don't Cry Sister' (Cale)
First recorded by Cale in 1979 for *5*, this sharp remake is a highlight of *The Road to Escondido*, with massed background vocals, a slight reggae accent, and some terrific guitar playing.

'Last Will and Testament' (Cale)
Tough lead guitar and swirling Hammond colour a straight I-IV-V blues song with J. J. and Eric singing in unison.

'Who Am I Telling You?' (Cale)
Listen to this one on headphones for the gorgeous production. Eric's and J.J.'s brilliant lead vocals are closely miked, and Derek Trucks adds some simple but very sweet slide guitar. The chemistry between the two men is very evident. The live version on 2016's *Live in San Diego*, recorded in 2007, is even better.

'Ride the River' (Cale)
Massed guitars and joint lead vocals colour perhaps the most successful collaboration on the album – the country chord changes and powerful guitar solos with deep reverb add variety. The production is impeccable.

Other Contemporary Tracks
'Isn't It A Pity' (Harrison)
Performed by Eric at the Concert for George in 2002, this brilliant George

Harrison song was added to Eric's concert tour setlist in 2007-2009. The recording from the 2007 Crossroads Festival is awe-inspiringly beautiful.

'Every Time I Sing the Blues' (Hambridge, Nicholson)

This is a scintillating duet between Eric Clapton and Buddy Guy from Guy's 2008 album *Skin Deep*. It has a deep groove, with Clapton and Guy trading vocals and lead guitar brilliantly. Eric drops in a quote from 'All Your Love' from the John Mayall *Beano* album near the end.

Clapton (2010)

Personnel:
Eric Clapton: vocals, guitar, mandolin
Doyle Bramhall II: guitar, vocals
Walt Richmond: keyboards
Willie Weeks: bass, double bass
Jim Keltner: drums
with

J. J. Cale: guitar, vocals on 'River Runs Deep', 'That's No Way to Get Along', 'Everything Will Be Alright'
Sheryl Crow: vocals on 'Diamonds Made from Rain'
Nikka Costa: backing vocals on 'Rocking Chair', 'Diamonds Made from Rain' and 'Run Back to Your Side'
Terry Evans, Willie Green, Jr and Arnold McCuller: backing vocals on 'Judgement Day' and 'That's No Way to Get Along'
Lynn Mabry and Debra Parsons: backing vocals on 'Diamonds Made from Rain' and 'Run Back to Your Side'
Steve Riley: accordion on 'That's No Way to Get Along'
Paul Carrack: Hammond organ on 'Everything Will Be Alright'
Derek Trucks: slide guitar on 'Rocking Chair', guitar on 'River Runs Deep'
Greg Leisz: pedal steel guitar on 'River Runs Deep'
James Poyser: Hammond organ on 'River Runs Deep', 'That's No Way to Get Along'
Allen Toussaint: piano on 'My Very Good Friend the Milkman' and 'When Somebody Thinks You're Wonderful'
Chris Severan: double bass on 'My Very Good Friend the Milkman' and 'When Somebody Thinks You're Wonderful'
Herman Labeaux: drums on 'My Very Good Friend the Milkman' and 'When Somebody Thinks You're Wonderful'
Troy Andrews, Matt Pyreem, Michael White: horns on 'My Very Good Friend the Milkman' and 'When Somebody Thinks You're Wonderful'
Sereca Henderson: organ on 'Diamonds Made from Rain'
Abe Laboriel Jr: drums on 'Rocking Chair', 'Autumn Leaves'
Jeremy Stacey: drums on 'River Runs Deep' and 'Diamonds Made from Rain'
Justin Stanley: drums on 'River Runs Deep'; percussion on 'That's No Way To get Along'
Cayetano 'Tanio' Hingle: percussion on 'My Very Good Friend the Milkman' and 'When Somebody Thinks You're Wonderful'; clarinet on 'That's No Way to Get Along'
Neal Sugarman, Leon Michaels, Thomas Brenneck: horns on 'River Runs Deep'
Kim Wilson: harmonica on 'Judgement Day' and 'Can't Hold Out Much Longer'
Wynton Marsalis: trumpet on 'How Deep Is the Ocean', 'My Very Good Friend the Milkman' and 'When Somebody Thinks You're Wonderful'
Clarenee Slaughter, Bruce Brackman, Edward Lee, Tim Callagan, Dan Ostreicher: horns on 'That's No Way to Get Along'

Sherrell Chenier Mouton: washboard on 'That's No Way to Get Along'
Tim Izo Orindgreff, Elizabeth Lea and Printz Board: trumpet on 'Everything Will Be Alright' and 'Diamonds Made from Rain'
The London Session Orchestra
Recorded 2009-2010 at Ocean Way, Los Angeles and Piety Street Studios, New Orleans. Produced by Eric Clapton and Doyle Bramhall II. 'Diamonds Made from Rain' co-produced by Justin Stanley. Released September 2010.
Highest chart positions: UK: 7, US: 6

Eric Clapton's important influences are easy to list: Robert Johnson, Buddy Guy, J. J. Cale, Muddy Waters, B.B. King, Ray Charles. With *Clapton* we can add, perhaps surprisingly: Fats Waller, Johnny Mercer, Hoagy Carmichael and Irving Berlin. Eric, in a contemporary press release:

> Singing songs such as 'Autumn Leaves' brings a whole other set of challenges that you hadn't thought about having to deal with. Like being able to sing the words like they mean something to you. So I have to then go inside the song and figure out a way to interpret it in a way that doesn't sound fake and just like any other old cover. Interpreting a song can be harder than writing one. It can be tough to make an old song come to life. I never liked young kids' music. I like old people's music.

Clapton is a roots album: sprightly, diverse, and seemingly effortless. Rather than the hard blues sound of *From the Cradle*, or the sleepy afternoon of *The Road to Escondido*, we have mature, considered selection of songs, mostly from before the rock 'n' roll era. Guests include Sheryl Crow, Allen Toussaint, Steve Winwood, Wynton Marsalis, Derek Trucks, Kim Wilson and Trombone Shorty. The rhythm section is anchored by keyboardist Walt Richmond, bassist Willie Weeks, and drummer Jim Keltner, and Doyle Bramhall II receives his first co-producer credit on an Eric Clapton album. He brought in his friend Justin Stanley, who had worked with Beck. Stanley engineered the album, and both co-wrote and co-produced the fabulous ballad 'Diamonds Made from Rain'.

According to contemporary interviews, *Clapton* was originally planned as a double album. It's unclear how far that idea progressed, but there are four excellent bonus tracks available in various formats of the album. These are all pure blues tracks that would have given the album a different feeling if included in the running order.

'Travelin' Alone' (Jackson)
A slinky, unnerving groove drives a magnificent song by Texas blues guitarist Lil' Son Jackson, first released in 1952. Once again, Clapton surprises with this new twist on an old-style – a warm, saturated guitar tone and touch of Cream swagger. Eric in 2010:

I'd always admired Lil' Son Jackson. And then I heard this one track by him, 'Travelin' Alone', that I thought was like nothing else he'd ever done. I thought: 'I've got to do that.'

'Rocking Chair' (Carmichael)
A blues arrangement of a popular Hoagy Carmichael song from 1929, perhaps best associated with Louis Armstrong. The short slide guitar solo adds sweet phrases by Derek Trucks. The song's simple, effective arrangement suits Clapton perfectly.

'River Runs Deep' (Cale)
The first of three songs featuring Cale on vocals and/or guitar. These are all very much in the style of *The Road to Escondido*. The production here is still lethargic: it hits a slow groove and stays there. The swooping swings and tough horn section lift the song, but it's a long, sluggish six minutes.

'Judgement Day' (Pryor)
A gentle but playful Chicago blues, written by harmonica maestro Snooky Pryor. The backing vocals by Terry Evans, Willie Green, Jr. and Arnold McCuller hark back to The Impressions' work on *Pilgrim*. The Fabulous Thunderbirds' Kim Wilson lets loose on harmonica.

'How Deep Is the Ocean' (Berlin)
'How Deep Is the Ocean' was written by Irving Berlin in 1932. It has been recorded by the likes of Chet Baker, Nat King Cole, Frank Sinatra, Peggy Lee and Charlie Parker. Clapton's vocal is 100% earnest, sensual and warm. Add acoustic guitar, mellow piano, clean-sounding electric guitar, strings and Wynton Marsalis to a delicious recipe.

'My Very Good Friend the Milkman' (Burke, Spina)
Recorded in New Orleans with Allen Toussaint and his band in full horn-laden N'Awlins style. This 1935 Fats Waller song is a great deal of fun, although casual listeners to Clapton's oeuvre might be startled by the style and delivery, which is far, far away from 'Layla' and 'Wonderful Tonight'. Paul McCartney recorded this song for his 2012 album *Kisses on the Bottom*.

'Can't Hold Out Much Longer' (Jacobs)
Dirty blues by Little Walter, probably the most influential blues harmonica player of them all. Kim Wilson's harmonica battles with an exhilarating Clapton guitar solo.

'That's No Way to Get Along' (Wilkins)
A call-and-response New Orleans collaboration with J. J. Cale on a new version

of the Robert Wilkins' 1930s blues number, recorded by The Rolling Stones as 'Prodigal Son' in 1968. Eric to *Mojo* in 2010:

> When I started singing it, J. J. started to repeat the line. I thought, 'What's he doing?' I thought he'd sing with me – but this was J. J. putting the New Orleans thing into it, and it was perfect. I learned from J. J. that it's okay if I sing very quietly. That's almost like not having to try to sing. You can have Ray Charles, who can do all kinds of things with his voice. Then you've got J. J. at the other end of the spectrum – he creates exactly the same amount of emotional capacity in a very minimal way. So there are different ways to do it.

Clapton is happy just to sing and play with J. J. Cale: the lead guitar solos are by Doyle Bramhall II.

'Everything Will Be Alright' (Cale)
A nice, easy, rolling J. J. Cale song, with the song's author on vocals. There is a lovely string and horn arrangement and a loose swing to 'Everything Will Be Alright', with a nimble guitar solo and Paul Carrack's Hammond underpinning everything.

'Diamonds Made from Rain' (Bramhall, Costa, Stanley)
A torch ballad written by Doyle Bramhall II with co-producer Justin Stanley and his wife, US R'n'B singer-songwriter Nikka Costa. It's a very good song, with a great vocal and an uplifting chorus. It's right at home amongst the older and/or rootsier selection on the rest of *Clapton*.

The production is exquisite, with swelling strings, Walt Richmond's flowing piano, and a brilliant, economic closing guitar solo.

'Diamonds Made from Rain' features Clapton's former flame Sheryl Crow on harmony vocals. The pair had a brief affair in the late 1990s, and it is rumoured she wrote her song 'My Favourite Mistake' about him.

'When Somebody Thinks You're Wonderful' (Woods)
This Tin Pan Alley standard from 1935 was written by Harry Woods and is most associated with Fats Waller. Clapton goes full-on New Orleans jazz, with swinging drumming from Herman Labeaux, dancing pianos from Walt Richmond and Allen Toussaint, and the peerless playing of Wynton Marsalis. Trombone, tuba and clarinet add to a rich arrangement. This song was added to Eric's live set and performed on *Later With Jools Holland* in November 2010.

'Hard Times Blues' (Hardin)
In which God plays mandolin on a lop-sided blues first cut in 1935 by the obscure St. Louis singer Lane Hardin. Doyle Bramhall II takes the slide solo.

'Run Back to Your Side' (Bramhall, Clapton)

A gravelly blues rocker featuring swinging groove and a forceful vocal, with Clapton, Doyle Bramhall and Derek Trucks playing a catchy riff. The three guitarists take turns playing lead, trading slide licks in an exhilarating central section.

'Autumn Leaves' (Kosma, Mercer, Prévert)

'Autumn Leaves' is a pop standard, covered by dozens of artists ranging from Edith Piaf to Nat King Cole. It's a Johnny Mercer lyric based on the French composition 'Les Feuilles Mortes'.

Eric Clapton's arrangement takes a muted instrumental backing, adds a gorgeous string arrangement, a hushed vocal, and two shining guitar solos, the second of which is remarkable. Clapton's perfect touch and very subtle choice of notes and intervals explain why his legend as the greatest British blues guitarist is secure.

This song choice is not at all what you might expect from Eric Clapton, but it's a work of genius, nevertheless.

Other Contemporary Tracks
'You Better Watch Yourself' (Guy)

This Buddy Guy track sounds like a fun warm-up rather than a serious attempt at a recording. Kim Wilson's blazing harmonica is the dominant instrument. Clapton had previously released a live version in 1991.

Released a bonus track on the ericclapton.com Deluxe Limited Edition of *Clapton*.

'Take a Little Walk with Me' (Lockwood)

A straight mid-paced rewrite of 'Sweet Home Chicago', originally by Robert Lockwood Jr, and also recorded by Otis Spann. Eric's arrangement is pure Chicago blues.

Released on the Barnes and Noble and Best Buy versions of *Clapton*.

'I Was Fooled' (Williams)

A Billy Boy Arnold song released in 1955 as the B-side of 'I Wish You Would', later recorded by The Yardbirds as their debut single in 1964. Eric provides a straight cover with a light touch.

Released as a bonus track on the iTunes version of *Clapton*, this is fresh and enjoyable.

'Midnight Hour Blues' (Carr, Blackwell)

Clapton had recorded two of Leroy Carr's songs on *From the Cradle* and would tackle a fourth on *I Still Do*. This is a gentle electric blues, reminiscent of Leadbelly's 'Alberta'.

Released as a bonus track on the Amazon.com version of *Clapton*.

Old Sock (2013)

Personnel:
Eric Clapton: lead vocals, electric guitar, acoustic guitar, twelve-string guitar, dobro, mandolin
Doyle Bramhall II: electric guitar, acoustic guitar, slide guitar, mandolin, backing vocals
Greg Leisz: pedal steel guitar, mandolin
Tim Carmon: organ
Simon Climie: acoustic piano, percussion
Frank Marocco: accordion
Walt Richmond, Matt Rollings, Chris Stainton: keyboards
Justin Stanley: keyboards, drums
Willie Weeks: bass
Matt Chamberlain, Steve Gadd, Jim Keltner, Abe Laboriel Jr and Henry Spinetti: drums
Gabe Witcher: fiddle
Stephen 'Doc' Kupka, Joseph Sublett, Nicholas Lane, Sal Cracchiolo: horns
Sharon White, Michelle John, Julie Clapton, Ella Clapton, Sophie Clapton, Nikka Costa, Wendy Moten, Lisa Vaughan: backing vocals
Taj Mahal: banjo and harmonica on 'Further on Down the Road'
J. J. Cale: guitar and vocals on 'Angel'
Steve Winwood: Hammond B3 organ on 'Still Got the Blues'
Paul McCartney: upright bass and backing vocals on 'All of Me'
Chaka Khan: guest vocals on 'Gotta Get Over'.
Recorded 2012-2013. Produced by Eric Clapton, Doyle Bramhall II, Justin Stanley and Simon Climie. Released March 2013.
Highest chart positions: UK: 13, US: 20

Old Sock revisits the successful formula set by *Clapton*: a comfortable, undemanding exploration of vintage folk, blues, soul, and country and reggae, seasoned with two American Songbook classics and new material written by Clapton's band. Perhaps only Eric Clapton could release an album by writers as diverse as Leadbelly, J. J. Cale, Peter Tosh, George Gershwin, Hank Snow, Gary Moore and Taj Mahal. In truth, despite a strong first half, the album tails off, closing with four indifferent songs.

With his Warner Brothers contract expired, *Old Sock* was released through the independent Bushbranch Records/Surfdog Records label.

'Further On Down the Road' (Mahal, Davis)
A delightful, relaxed reggae, almost a note-for-note copy of the original, first released by Taj Mahal as 'Farther On Down the Road (You Will Accompany Me)' in 1969. It suits Clapton perfectly and sets out this album's objectives from the start: a gentle stroll through some of Clapton's favourite songs by other artists.

The song's co-writer offers a sparkling harmonica solo.

{Eric Clapton solo ... *On Track*}

'Angel' (Cale)

An unreleased J. J. Cale song that was started during the joint sessions with J. J. Cale for the Clapton album in 2009-2010. Eric, in a song-by-song commentary released with some versions of the album:

> When we [finished] *Clapton*, we had [unused] tracks in the can. I had about three songs, maybe more, actually, that I thought were up to scratch. 'Angel' was one of them. We'd never really resolved it, so we kinda re-did it again. But we had JJ's voice on there and everything. And so it was another homage.

It's snappier than many other Cale songs, and Clapton's recording is beautifully produced. Cale's voice supports Eric's in the chorus, backed up by female backing vocals, shiny pedal steel, and some nice guitar picking.

Cale died four months after the release of *Old Sock*.

'The Folks Who Live on the Hill' (Hammerstein, Kern)

A popular song from 1937, written by Oscar Hammerstein II and Jerome Kern for the film *High, Wide, and Handsome*. It was also recorded by Bing Crosby, Guy Lombardo and Peggy Lee. As with 'Autumn Leaves', 'Our Love Is Here to Stay' and 'When Somebody Thinks You're Wonderful', this song, with its sincere vocals and syrupy strings, will either delight or infuriate listeners: has Eric lost it, or, at 67, has he earned the right to sing whatever he pleases? You decide.

'Gotta Get Over' (Bramhall, Stanley, Costa)

'Gotta Get Over' is a powerful, vigorous, funky rock song with a distinctive guitar riff and gospel-influenced chorus. Chaka Khan adds her distinctive backing vocals to Eric's gritty lead.

'Till Your Well Runs Dry' (Tosh)

'Till Your Well Runs Dry' has a superb Clapton vocal, colouring the bluesy medium tempo verses. The song has an infectious reggae lilt on the chorus and a short, sweet guitar solo.

Peter Tosh's original is on his 1976 album *Legalize It*. Some sources suggest that Eric played on the sessions for *Legalize It*. The 2011 re-release includes an 'original Jamaican mix' of 'Till Your Well Runs Dry', which either has Eric's playing or someone doing a very good take-off.

'All of Me' (Marks, Simons)

A playful jazz-tinted duet featuring one P. McCartney of Allerton, some tinkling barroom piano, and fat slices of slide guitar. The song dates from 1931, as is perhaps best known in versions by Louis Armstrong, Frank Sinatra, Johnny Ray, Billie Holiday and Willie Nelson.

'Born to Lose' (Daffan)

A country song written by Ted Daffan, recorded by Ray Charles for his 1962 album *Modern Sounds in Country and Western Music*. This the most traditional-sounding country sound Clapton has yet produced, with wailing pedal steel, trilling fiddle, and the welcome return of some delightful dobro.

'Still Got the Blues' (Moore)

Northern Irish guitar wizard Gary Moore recorded *Still Got the Blues*, a glossy set of blues originals and covers, in 1990. Moore to *Louder Sound* in 2007:

> There was a great blues scene in Belfast. All these guitar players used to come up from Cork, like Rory Gallagher. And then we heard about British blues. The first time I heard Eric Clapton play guitar, it changed my life. Something very profound happened when I heard that record [*Bluesbreakers With Eric Clapton*]. Within two seconds of the opening track, I was blown away. The guitar sound itself was so different. You could hear the blues in it, but prior to that, the guitar had been very staid, very polite. Just listen to the early Beatles and The Shadows to see what I mean. They were great, but Eric Clapton transcended it completely.

Moore formed the band BBM in 1993, reuniting Jack Bruce and Ginger Baker to record new material and play old Cream songs such as 'Deserted Cities of the Heart', 'I Feel Free', and 'Politician'.

'Still Got the Blues' is one of Moore's signature songs. Clapton takes it slowly and regretfully, with a dark, slightly jazzy arrangement, a warm, rich vocal, crooning strings, gently picked acoustic guitar, and Steve Winwood's swirling Hammond organ. The electric guitar solo that plays out the song simply sobs the blues.

Moore had died in February 2011, and Clapton's tribute would no doubt have made Gary Moore a proud man. Clapton played the song live in 2011.

'Goodnight Irene' (Ledbetter)

The album fizzles out with four less inspired efforts. The first of these 'Goodnight Irene' is a folk classic first recorded by Leadbelly in 1933. It was a big hit for The Weavers in 1950 and has been recorded by many artists over the years – including Eric Clapton on Chas and Dave's December 1982 TV special. Clapton and old friend Albert Lee performed 'Goodnight Irene' at Hodges' memorial concert at the Shepherd's Bush Empire in 2018. This version pairs Clapton's acoustic guitar with dobro and fiddle.

'Your One and Only Man' (Redding)

An Otis Redding B-side from late 1964, also released on *The Great Otis Redding Sings Soul Ballads* in March 1965. Clapton's confident version is given a reggae twist and a bluesy growl but dilutes the sheer bravura of the original.

'Every Little Thing' (Bramhall, Stanley, Costa)
Released as a single, May 2013. Did not chart.

An irritatingly catchy song written for Clapton by Doyle Bramhall, Justin Stanley and Nikki Costa. Eric in the song-by-song commentary for the album:

> It's principally for me to sing for the family. It's about our family. It's about my family. He [Bramhall] just thought I could apply it to that as a source of inspiration and then, you know, we got to this thing of, well, let's get them on there. Get the kids on there. And if you listen, they're on the end. I think it's lovely.

Whilst we cannot doubt the sincerity, do we really need to hear his kids singing?
The download single includes two remixes by Damian and Stephen Marley. These add a nice dub feel.

'Our Love Is Here to Stay' (Gershwin, Gershwin)
A popular song and jazz standard composed by George and Ira Gershwin for the film *The Goldwyn Follies* (1938). 'Love Is Here to Stay' was George Gershwin's last musical composition before his death. The song had further popularity when sung by Gene Kelly in the film *An American in Paris* (1951) and by Harry Connick Jr in *When Harry Met Sally ...* (1989). It's been recorded by Ella Fitzgerald, Billie Holiday, Dinah Washington, Frank Sinatra, Ray Charles and Diana Ross. I'm not sure whether we needed another variant on 'Autumn Leaves', but we got one anyway.

Other Contemporary Tracks
'No Sympathy' (Tosh)
Written and originally recorded by Peter Tosh for his 1976 debut solo album, *Legalize It*. 'No Sympathy' is the fourth song that Clapton has covered from the album. Clapton adds some vicious wah-wah guitar to this tough reggae song.
The recording was released online and made available as part of a deluxe edition of *Old Sock,* which had a custom linen-covered book, and a USB Card with hi-res audio files of all songs, with this track as a bonus.

'Tempted' (Tilbrook, Difford)
'How Long' (Carrack)
Paul Carrack's spotlight songs in Eric's live sets in 2013-2014, both hit songs for Carrack in previous bands. 'Tempted' is Squeeze's hit single from 1981, and 'How Long' was a 1975 hit for Ace.

'High Time We Went' (Cocker, Stainton)
Eric's usual encore number since 2013, sung by Paul Carrack. It was written by Joe Cocker, and Clapton's long-time band member Chris Stainton.

The Breeze: An Appreciation of J. J. Cale (2014)

Personnel:
Eric Clapton: guitars, lead and backing vocals, dobro
Walt Richmond: keyboards
Simon Climie: programming, percussion, background vocals on 'Songbird'
Nathan East: bass
Jim Keltner: drums
James Cruce, Jim Karstein, Jamie Oldaker and David Teegarden: additional drums
Satnam Ramgotra: tablas
Tom Petty: vocals on 'Rock and Roll Records', 'I Got the Same Old Blues' and 'The Old Man and Me'
Mark Knopfler: guitar, vocals on 'Someday' and 'Train to Nowhere'
John Mayer: guitar, vocals on 'Lies', 'Magnolia' and 'Don't Wait'
Willie Nelson: guitar, vocals on 'Songbird' and 'Starbound'
Don White: guitar, vocals on 'Someday', 'Sensitive Kind', 'I'll Be There (If You Ever Want Me)' and 'Train to Nowhere'
Reggie Young: guitar on 'Rock and Roll Records', 'Cajun Moon' and 'I Got the Same Old Blues'
Derek Trucks: guitar on 'Starbound' and 'Crying Eyes'
Albert Lee: guitar on 'Call Me the Breeze' and 'I'll Be There (If You Ever Want Me)'
David Lindley: guitar on 'Songbird' and 'Crying Eyes'
Don Preston: guitar on 'Someday' and 'Train to Nowhere'
Christine Lakeland: guitar on 'Someday', vocals on 'Crying Eyes'
Doyle Bramhall II: guitar on 'Since You Said Goodbye'
Greg Leisz: pedal steel guitar on 'The Old Man and Me' and 'Starbound'
Jimmy Markham: harmonica on 'Train to Nowhere'
Mickey Raphael: harmonica on 'Someday', 'Songbird' and 'Starbound'
Michelle John and Sharon White: background vocals on 'Lies', 'Sensitive Kind', 'Songbird' and 'Train to Nowhere'.
Recorded 2013-2014 in Columbus, New York, Nashville, Los Angeles and London.
Produced by Eric Clapton and Simon Climie. Released July 2014.
Highest chart positions: UK:3, US: 2

J. J. Cale died on 26 July 2013, aged 74. Eric Clapton flew to Los Angeles for the funeral, and during the flight, started to map out ideas for a memorial album to celebrate Cale's life and work. Eric to *Uncut* in 2015:

I was just going to do it on my own, but then I met someone at the funeral called Don White. There were very few people there: Jim Keltner was there, and [Cale's wife] Christine, and this guy Don White. He said, 'You wouldn't know about me, but I gave John his first job as a guitar player.' So I thought, 'I can't do this on my own, I have to let people like this into the project.' He was the first person I asked, and it just gathered momentum from there. I met Christine and [Cale's agent] Mike Kappus, and we paid our respects to one another and gave each other hugs.

I held back as much as I could, but as soon as I thought it was decent, I said, 'I'd like to make a record to pay tribute to John'. And they said, 'That would be great.'

Eric spoke at Cale's memorial service and said that he had two heroes: Robert Johnson and J. J. Cale. Eric, to *Uncut*:

We had made tracks in [Clapton's home studio in] Columbus on the computer, with me playing guitar and singing guide vocals, and we took it to LA and then put live musicians on. Then afterwards, we thought about Willie [Nelson], and so Simon went to Nashville and recorded Willie on site. We got Reggie Young to play, Derek Trucks to play, Albert Lee – anybody that I thought of who had a feeling for JJ. Then when we came back to England, I thought, 'Well, there's one person we have to ask, we'll need to go to his studio'. We went to British Grove, where Mark Knopfler has his place, and I asked him to sing two songs, and that was it. I thought, 'We've got it now.'

Lakeland, speaking to the *San Diego Tribune* in 2014:

Eric was very conscientious. He wanted to make sure I thought he was doing well with John's music ... He made me feel as if my opinion mattered, even if I didn't think that. It was a really nice feeling. He made me feel like my two cents worth was worth a whole lot more than two cents.

Clapton and his band play on all tracks. A-list guest performers include Tom Petty, Mark Knopfler, John Mayer and Willie Nelson. Guest musicians include Clapton's former drummer Jamie Oldaker and multi-instrumentalist session musician David Lindley, along with members of Cale's band.

Half of the songs come from Cale's 1974 album *Okie*. Despite the familiarity of the material, or perhaps because of it, *The Breeze* is a fine tribute, loose and laid-back. It won't win over casual listeners, but that's not the point.

***The Breeze* was a major hit, reaching the top three in the UK and the US. Clapton to the *San Diego Tribune*:**

As a musician, I've analyzed it and analyzed it. I've looked at his stuff from every possible angle – from enjoyment to inspiration, to being investigative – to find out how he does it. And I still don't get all the lyrics half the time! I'm still not sure what he's singing about, and that fascinates me ... that he was that unconcerned about getting his message across. I always believed he did it purely for himself, and that's the greatest enjoyment of all.

'Call Me the Breeze' (Cale)

At first, it feels a little odd hearing a song that's associated as much with Lynyrd Skynyrd as J. J. Cale. Cale's original opens his 1972 debut album, and this arrangement is a carbon copy, right down to the drum machine. Clapton's vocals are as close to Cale's as to be almost indistinguishable, but Albert Lee makes a welcome return, adding some perfect country picking. If you want to hear how Lynyrd Skynyrd tackle this, then pull out *Second Helping* or *One More From the Road*.

'Rock and Roll Records' (Cale)
Tom Petty, an artist who understood American roots music better than most, is an ideal choice to sing Cale's 'Rock and Roll Records', originally from *Okie* (1974). Eric in 2014:

> We started with Tom. He made it really clear that he wanted to do something.

Clapton and Petty sing in close harmony and the song swaggers gently.

'Someday' (Cale, Richmond)
A previously unheard Cale original, 'Someday' suits Mark Knopfler well – after all, he based much of his early career on Cale's sound. Knopfler's distinctive guitar and vocals are given lots of space here, to great effect.

'Lies' (Cale)
Very close to Cale's original in tempo and arrangement, this version of *Lies* (from *Really*, 1972) has some delicate picking from Clapton, and harmonised lead vocals from Clapton and John Mayer.

> 'Lies', sung with John Mayer, could have benefited from the charismatic delivery of a vet like Dr John or Leon Russell.
> Patrick Doyle, *Rolling Stone*, 29 July 2014

'Sensitive Kind' (Cale)
Surely one of J. J. Cale's best songs, this slow, swampy take of 'Sensitive Kind' from 5 (1979) has a smartly judged, perfectly phrased solo from Clapton, and a warm, deep lead vocal by Don White. I think White also provides some of the J. J. Cale-style lead guitar, too.
Santana's version from *Zebop!* (1981) is worth a listen.

'Cajun Moon' (Cale)
This is a close copy of Cale's original. Although only Eric is credited as vocalist here, there's another singer duetting. It doesn't sound like double-tracking.
'Cajun Moon' has also been recorded by Herbie Mann (1976), country-rockers Poco (1982) and, in Cale's personal favourite, by Randy Crawford (1995).

'Magnolia' (Cale)
One of the album's many highlights, this slow-burning song features wunderkind blues-rock singer John Mayer. Eric in 2014:

I heard that John Mayer was on YouTube doing 'Call Me the Breeze', and so we asked him. He's ideal for this because we need someone with that kind of energy, and he's a good interpreter. We went into the studio in New York with the tracks, and he got the three songs in two hours or something like that, first and second takes. Needed no direction whatsoever.

The arrangement is fabulous, with quivering guitar fills, silky organ, and Mayer's laid back, easy vocals.

'I Got the Same Old Blues' (Cale)

'I Got the Same Old Blues' is one of J. J. Cale's most familiar songs. Other versions of this song are worth hearing, especially those by Captain Beefheart (*Bluejeans and Moonbeams*, 1974) and Lynyrd Skynyrd (*Gimme Back My Bullets*, 1976).

Tom Petty's vocals are pure J. J. Cale – you need to listen hard to realise who's actually singing. Clapton's guitar is strong, distorted and distinctive. Session ace Reggie Young, who played on Cale's original, adds some tasty licks of his own.

'Songbird' (Cale)

'Songbird' is an unheard Cale song perfectly suited to Willie Nelson's cracked baritone. The arrangement is mostly acoustic – Eric gets out his dobro, and David Lindley adds acoustic guitar.

'Since You Said Goodbye' (Cale)

'Since You Said Goodbye' was recorded by J. J. Cale in 1973 but remained unreleased until 2007. Clapton's confident vocals are matched by Doyle Bramhall's sweet electric slide guitar.

'I'll Be There (If You Ever Want Me)' (Price, Gabbard)

'I'll Be There (If You Ever Want Me)' was a big country hit for Ray Price in 1954. J. J. Cale covered this on his third album *Okie* (1974).

Don White howls the Burrito Brothers-style stomper 'I'll Be There', grooving like a high-noon drive through the Baja desert.
Patrick Doyle, *Rolling Stone,* 29 July 2014

White's vocals are excellent, Eric plays brilliant dobro and sings harmonies, and Albert Lee's guitar leads are unmistakable.

'The Old Man and Me' (Cale)

Another gruff Tom Petty vocal, this time sweetened by sometime Clapton band member Greg Leisz on pedal steel guitar.

'Train to Nowhere' (Cale)
The third unheard Cale original, which perhaps confirms just how much Mark Knopfler owes to J. J. Cale, as his patent boogie shuffle guitar patterns underpin the song. Knopfler and Don White share vocals.

'Starbound' (Cale)
One of the less successful songs on the album: Willie Nelson never quite gets his idiosyncratic vocal style around this two-minute song. In compensation, both Derek Trucks and Greg Leisz add gorgeous slide guitar and pedal steel.

'Don't Wait' (Cale, Lakeland)
The toughest song here, with Clapton's raw riffery opening the song and punching through the verses. Lead vocals are by Eric Clapton and John Mayer in J. J. Cale's familiar close-harmony style.

'Crying Eyes' (Cale)
Cale's wife and muse Christine Lakeland joins Eric to sing the closing song from 1972's *Naturally*. Both David Lindley and Derek Trucks add sharp slide guitar solos. Bassist Nathan East to the *San Diego Tribune*:

> There were definitely a few tears flowing during the session for 'Crying Eyes'. Eric wanted to make sure Christine was happy ... He wanted to keep J.J.'s music alive in as pure a fashion as it could be recorded.

Other Contemporary Songs
'Don't Go to Strangers' (Cale)
A track from J. J. Cale's debut album *Naturally* performed in concert just twice as the opening song on 13 and 14 November 2013 at the Event Halle, Basel, Switzerland. Eric also sang 'Since You Said Goodbye', 'After Midnight', 'Call Me the Breeze' and 'Cocaine'. It's likely that 'Don't Go to Strangers' was recorded as part of the sessions for *The Breeze*. Clapton in 2014:

> In two weeks, we cut something like 24 (songs) ... It was fast and furious and driven by the energy we had.

Perhaps these songs will see release one day.

I Still Do (2016)

Personnel:
Eric Clapton: guitar, tambourine, lead vocals
Paul Brady: acoustic guitar, backing vocals
Andy Fairweather Low: acoustic guitar, electric guitar, backing vocals
Simon Climie: acoustic guitar, electric guitar, keyboards
Walt Richmond, Chris Stainton: keyboards
Paul Carrack: Hammond organ, backing vocals
Dirk Powell: accordion, mandolin, backing vocals
Dave Bronze: bass
Henry Spinetti: drums, percussion
Ethan Johns: percussion
Michelle John and Sharon White: backing vocals
Ed Sheeran: acoustic guitar, backing vocals on 'I Will Be There'.
Recorded October – December 2015 at British Grove Studios, London.
Produced by Glyn Johns.
Released May 2016. Highest chart positions: UK: 6, US: 6.

With *I Still Do*, Eric Clapton's solo career comes full circle. The commercial sheen of the 1980s, the polished acoustic Yuppie music and hard blues of the 1990s, the slick R'n'B stylings of the 2000s, and the roots homages of the 2010s have all been worked through. *I Still Do* returns Clapton to the warm, organic sounds of *Slowhand* and *Backless*. Not coincidentally, *I Still Do* reunites Clapton with the producer of those albums, Glyn Johns.

> He approached me about doing the record. I wrote a book [*Sound Man*] a couple of years ago in which I stated how I missed him as a pal – because when he stopped drinking, he stopped seeing all the people he'd hang out with, which is a normal thing for alcoholics. And whereas I completely understood the reasons, selfishly I missed him as a mate. So he rang me and said: 'What are you talking about? Of course I'm still your mate!' And we had lunch a couple of times and he said: 'Let's make a record.' So we did. There are three traditional blues songs on the record. It's an extremely eclectic mix. There's 'Catch the Blues', which is Latin American, a couple of J. J. Cale numbers, a very early gospel song, and 'I'll Be Seeing You' which is not bluesy in the least. But of course he tips his hat to the blues, because that's what he is – a bluesman.

I Still Do is an assured and poised album, recorded in London at British Grove Studios – owned by Clapton's old pal Mark Knopfler. The album was recorded to 16-track tape, with the musicians playing together in the same room, usually in three or four takes. It was coloured by the inevitable consequences of ageing. Clapton, interviewed by *Louder Sound* in 2016:

I've had quite a lot of pain over the last year. It started with lower back pain and turned into what they call peripheral neuropathy, which is where you feel like you have electric shocks going down your leg. And I've had to figure out how to deal with some other things from getting old.

As a result of the treatment for his ailments, Clapton contracted a severe case of eczema, just as recording had commenced. Glyn Johns:

And that would have been alright, except that it went to his hands, and so he found it incredibly difficult to play because the skin was shredding off them. It drove him nuts not to be able to play. But that's why there's bottleneck/slide on the record because on some days, he couldn't play any other way.

Clapton in 2016:

It was a nightmare. I started thinking that it was psychosomatic, that maybe I was nervous. And maybe I was. Who knows? I had full-body eczema and it ended up on my hands. I had to wear mittens with band-aids around the hands and played a lot of slide [guitar] as a result.

The sleeve of the album shows Clapton's heavily bandaged hands.

[The album's title] came from something a relative – my old aunty – said shortly before she passed away. I was talking to her about when I was a kid and thanking her for being kind, and she said: 'I liked you. And I still do.' And I thought, well, that's as good as it gets. So I kind of made a mental note and thought: 'I'll use that.'

I Still Do reached a very credible number six in both the UK and US – not bad for the man's twenty-third solo album.

At around this time, Clapton recorded twenty minutes of beautiful new music for a documentary called *Three Days in Auschwitz*, a very personal film produced by Phillipe Mora, for whom Eric had provided the soundtrack for *Communion* in 1989. *Three Days in Auschwitz* marries electric and acoustic guitar to orchestral strings, much in the vein of Michael Kamen's unreleased 'Concerto for Electric Guitar and Orchestra'. The documentary was released in September 2016.

Two years later, he released *Happy Xmas*, co-produced with Simon Climie. It includes covers of Christmas themed songs in a bluesy style and one new composition. The tracklist is 'White Christmas', 'Away in a Manger (Once in Royal David's City)', 'For Love on Christmas Day' (a new Clapton, Climie composition), 'Everyday Will Be Like a Holiday' (a William Bell song from 1967), 'Christmas Tears' (recorded by Freddie King in 1961, performed live by Clapton in 1998), 'Home for the Holidays' (written and recorded by Anthony Hamilton in 2014), 'Jingle Bells', 'Christmas in My Hometown' (a Sonny James song from 1954), 'It's Christmas' (another Anthony Hamilton song), 'Sentimental Moments' (from the 1955 film *We're No Angels*), 'Lonesome Christmas' (recorded by Lowell Fulson in 1951). 'Silent Night', 'Merry Christmas Baby' (recorded by Johnny Moore, Otis Redding, B. B. King and many others), 'Have Yourself a Merry Little Christmas' (viz Judy Garland), 'A Little Bit of Christmas Love' (by Memphis blues singer Rosco Gordon) and 'You Always Hurt the One You Love' (a US number one for The Mills Brothers in 1944 and a top twenty UK hit for Connie Francis in 1959). Eric's core band for this project was Doyle Bramhall II, Walt Richmond, Simon Climie, Tim Carmon, Nathan East and Jim Keltner, with session keyboardist Toby Baker and American fiddler Dirk Powell. Released October 2018. Highest chart positions: UK: 97, US: 84.

'Alabama Woman Blues' (Carr)
The accordion enters the blues lexicon. 'Alabama Woman Blues' is a stately Leroy Carr song, recorded as early as 1930. Clapton had performed the song live in 1993 and 2014. The slow-tempo, deep production and loads of rich slide guitar (a Gibson ES-335) on 'Alabama Woman Blues' heralds a more organic sound on *I Still Do*.

Clapton chose Carr's original version of 'Alabama Woman Blues' for a compilation cover CD to coincide with an interview in *Uncut* in May 2004.

'Can't Let You Do It' (Cale)
Released as a single, April 2016. Did not chart.

This rolling bluesy track is a cover of an unreleased song by J. J. Cale. Clapton to *Guitar World* in 2016:

I met up with [Cale's widow], Christine, and said, 'Is there anything laying about that I could maybe finish or work with?' I was very curious to know if there was a legacy. She said, 'Oh, there's some stuff. I'll make you some CDs.' She gave me two CDs a couple of days later with about 20 songs on each, so I had those locked up in a safe [laughs]. They're so precious to me. They're unreleased J. J. demos and some of them are really, really out there; others are the kind of thing you'd expect from J.J..

'Can't Let You Do It' and 'Somebody's Knockin'' both come from this cache. Clapton copies Cale's familiar double-tracked vocal style here, along with the general relaxed mood of a typical Cale track. Chris Stainton shines on piano, and the brilliant Henry Spinetti skips the beat along.

'I Will Be There' (Brady, O'Kane)
This gentle folk-pop-reggae love song was co-written by Irish singer Paul Brady and first appeared on Brady's 1995 album *Spirits Colliding*. Mary Black

released a popular version on her 1997 album *Shine*. One 'Angelo Mysterioso' is credited for acoustic guitar and vocals on this song. George Harrison used a near-identical pseudonym when he played on 'Badge', the tune he and Clapton wrote on Cream's 1969 album, *Goodbye,* and as a result, there was speculation that this was a track the former Beatle had left behind. Clapton told *Guitar World* the mystery collaborator wasn't Harrison:

> No, it's not George. Well, the thing is, the person wishes to remain anonymous. So we came to that arrangement, and we both thought it was the best idea, for one reason or another. And I can't even tell you that much. I'm sworn to secrecy, and I hope he is, too. But I quite liked it.

It's very obviously Ed Sheeran. Their voices work surprisingly well together. Eric in 2018:

> My kids listen to stuff and I try to keep up. They love Ed Sheeran. He's become a friend and I really admire what he does. And I'm grateful that he says nice things about me.

They performed 'I Will Be There' together in Japan in 2016. Eric returned the favour, adding a guitar solo to the song 'Dive' on Sheeran's 2017 album *Plus*.

'Spiral' (Clapton, Fairweather Low, Climie)
A tremendous, brooding Clapton original with an economic, insistent riff, a strong lead vocal and self-aware lyrics.

> You don't know how much this means
> To have this music in me
> I just keep playing these blues

'Spiral' has the first co-writing credit for Andy Fairweather Low on an Eric Clapton album. On this evidence, they should write together more often. Eric, interviewed on the DVD released with some versions of the album:

> I had this riff, and I was playing around with it with Andy. It wasn't a song, it was just a series of chord changes. We just started playing it ... to see what would emerge. It was born there, on the spot. And we recorded it live. It's quite abstract – it's about my compulsion to play, and my love for music.

'Catch the Blues' (Clapton)
Released as a single, May 2016. Did not chart.

A return to the Latin American of 'Signe' and 'Change the World', with a breezy double-tracked vocal and some growling wah-wah guitar flourishes.

There are even hints of Steely Dan in the smooth professionalism on display here. Listen on headphones. The mix is beautiful. Glyn Johns, on the *Old Sock* DVD:

> It's a great song. The rhythm section [Dave Bronze and Henry Spinetti] are astonishing, and I love the slide guitar playing on it. I think it's extraordinary.

'Cypress Grove' (James)
Deep, swampy blues, written by Skip James in 1931. Cream recorded James' 'I'm So Glad' on their debut album in 1966. The slow, off-kilter rhythm, powerful slide, and out-of-place accordion give this song an unusual, effective rhythm.

'Little Man, You've Had a Busy Day' (Sigler, Wayne, Hoffman)
Eric sings Perry Como? 'Little Man, You've Had a Busy Day' is an affecting lullaby, first recorded in 1934. Clapton's arrangement is vastly different to the light classic pop version recorded by Como, Bing Crosby and others. It comprises just acoustic guitar, electric guitar and double bass – like he's singing at the back of a blues bar – and has another great Clapton vocal. But who's he singing to? Perhaps his grandsons, Isaac and Theodore, born in 2014 and 2016?

'Stones in My Passway' (Johnson)
The twenty-third Robert Johnson song logged in Eric Clapton's long career. He had previously recorded this as a solo acoustic performance in a Santa Monica hotel room in 2004 for the *Sessions for Robert J* documentary. This 2016 version has the feeling of an impromptu jam session: it's loose and easy, with loud slide guitar and unusual instrumentation – booming bass drum, tinkling harmonica, mandolin and accordion.

'I Dreamed I Saw St. Augustine' (Dylan)
A very welcome cover of this 1967 Bob Dylan song, first released on *John Wesley Harding*, where it immediately precedes Dylan's original version of 'All Along the Watchtower'.

It has an organic, rootsy sound, very much like The Band's recordings from their early albums: double bass, accordion, acoustic guitar, piano, sharply picked and clean electric guitar, all recorded together in the same room. Lovely.

'I'll Be Alright' (traditional)
A slow two-step gospel, which has links to 'We Shall Overcome' and 'No Auction Block'. The slide guitar solo is a lesson in restraint. The stirring choir (composed of Clapton's band and backing singers) is subtly used and gives the song a real lift.

'Somebody's Knockin'' (Cale)
'Somebody's Knockin'' is another unheard J. J. Cale song, a wholly engaging slow, straightforward, gently swinging twelve-bar blues, with a warm lead vocal and some classic bluesy guitar licks. Yes, we've heard this type of song many times before, but the style fits Clapton so well, and the execution is so sublime that we should just sit back and enjoy it. 'Somebody's Knockin'' was performed live in 2015-2016: watch *Slowhand at 70* for a magnificent seven-minute version.

'I'll Be Seeing You' (Kahal, Fain)
'I'll Be Seeing You' was composed in 1938 by Irving Kahal and Sammy Fain and recorded by Bing Crosby, Billie Holiday and many others. It's Frank Sinatra's version that inspired Clapton here, as he told *Louder Sound* in 2016:

> It took me all this time to understand Frank Sinatra – that's been really difficult. And I think it might have something to do with the fact that he is so highly revered. And often, my response to that idolatry is to go, 'Nah' – to trash it and go looking for something more obscure. Because he was so familiar and popular. And bit by bit, I've had to come to terms with the fact that he was a genius. Frank Sinatra could actually really do deep emotional work, but I didn't want to admit it till the last couple of years.

Is it possible to interpret this song as a farewell? Eric on the *Old Sock* DVD:

> No, no. It's just a lovely song. A lot of people dropped off over the last couple of years, and I'm kind of singing to them. And it's not me saying goodbye to everyone who's still alive, I'm saying goodbye in that song to the people that I've had to let go. Not just famous people, but close family and friends and colleagues. This last couple of years have been extraordinary; maybe because I'm reaching that age where funerals become a weekly event. So I'm singing to them, really.

Other Contemporary Tracks
'Lonesome' (Clapton)
'Lonesome' distils many of Eric's tropes: 'Rollin' and Tumblin'' slide guitar, J. J. Cale-style vocals, female backing vocals, smart chord changes, rather cheesy lyrics.

'Lonesome' was released as a bonus track on the 'Denim Box' version of *I Still Do*.

'Freight Train' (Clapton)
A delightful Clapton original with a chugging rhythm, a slight bluegrass twist, and folky lyrics. This song shares a mood and title (but not melody or lyrics) with a folk-blues written by Elizabeth Cotten (1893 –1987). A 1956 recording of

Cotton's song by Chas McDevitt and Nancy Whiskey was a major hit in the UK and is credited as one of the main influences on the rise of skiffle.

Released as a bonus track on the 'Denim Box' version of *I Still Do*.

'Tribute to Jack Bruce' (Clapton)

Eric recorded a short acoustic piece following the death of Jack Bruce in October 2014, aged 71. He shared the song on his Facebook page in tribute, and the recording was played at Bruce's funeral. Although Clapton was unable to attend a concert in Bruce's honour, he donated the recording to the double album *Sunshine of Your Love: A Concert for Jack Bruce,* released in 2019.

'Stand and Deliver' (Morrison)

Released in December 2020, this straightforward blues, written by Van Morrison, benefits Morrison's Lockdown Financial Hardship Fund, which aims to assist musicians who are struggling amid the coronavirus pandemic.

'There are many of us who support Van and his endeavours to save live music; he is an inspiration,' Clapton said in a statement. 'We must stand up and be counted because we need to find a way out of this mess. The alternative is not worth thinking about. Live music might never recover.'

Whilst we agree with that statement, embarrassing anti-Government lyrics such as 'Is this a sovereign nation or just a police state? / You better look out, people, before it gets too late' and 'Stand and deliver / Dick Turpin wore a mask too' perhaps do not show these veteran musicians in the best light.

Live Albums and Live Recordings

Eric Clapton has released many live albums during his solo career: his natural milieu is the concert stage, and this has been well-represented over the years, as have his guest appearances with other artists.

In many ways, Clapton's first two solo concerts, held with an all-star backing band at the Rainbow Theatre in London on 13 January 1973, were a false start. Clapton's performance is cautious and often overshadowed by Steve Winwood, who takes much of the kudos here. Six songs were released on *Eric Clapton's Rainbow Concert* later that year. It was 'a recording of monolithic melancholy,' wrote Bud Scoppa in *Rolling Stone*. 'One might suppose that hard rock and despair are antithetical, but Clapton makes the union viable and compelling. But not fun.' The 1995 remastered edition rebuilds a complete set from the two shows that day.

It's worth mentioning here that these concerts marked the first public appearance of Clapton's famous black guitar. As he says in his memoirs:

> The guitar I chose to use was one I had built myself, a Fender Stratocaster I had nicknamed Blackie. In the early days, in spite of my admiration for both Buddy Holly and Buddy Guy, both Strat players, I had predominantly played a Gibson Les Paul. But one day, while on tour with the Dominos, I saw Steve Winwood with a white Strat and, inspired by him, I went into Sho-Bud in Nashville, and they had a stack of Strats in the back of the shop. They were completely out of fashion at the time, and I bought six of them for a song, no more than about a hundred dollars each. These vintage instruments would be worth about a hundred times that today. When I got home, I gave one to Steve, one to Pete Townshend, and another to George Harrison and kept the rest. I then took the other three and made one guitar out of them, using the best components of each.

Blackie was retired in 1985 and sold in 2004 for $959,500, setting the record for the world's most expensive guitar.

EC Was Here (1975), recorded in July and December 1974, presents Clapton in rude health as a supreme blues guitarist: 'Rambling on My Mind', 'Further On up the Road' and an astonishing 'Have You Ever Loved a Woman' are joined by two tracks from Blind Faith and a cover of Johnny Moore's 1945 hit 'Driftin''. On the vinyl album, this fades after 3.25 – on CD it's allowed to stretch to 11.43. The 2013 box set, *Give Me Strength-The '74-'75 Recordings,* includes an extended, remixed and remastered *EC Was Here*, expanded across two CDs, with numerous unissued extras such as versions of 'Layla', 'Crossroads' and 'Little Wing', and a remarkable, driven 23-minute medley of 'Eyesight to the Blind' and 'Why Does Love Got To Be So Sad?' A few other tracks from this same series of concerts are available on the 2004 deluxe edition of *461 Ocean Boulevard*.

The Bobby 'Blue' Bland song 'Further On Up the Road' was a regular encore number for Eric Clapton for ten years or more. A live version recorded with guest Freddie King in Dallas on 15 November 1976 was released on *Freddie King 1934-1976*. More famously, Clapton performed this song with The Band at their farewell concert in San Francisco on 26 November 1976. Clapton almost drops his guitar in the excitement of it all. The concert was filmed and recorded and given a theatrical release and triple live album, *The Last Waltz*, in 1978. Clapton also sings and plays on the ensemble finale of 'I Shall Be Released'. A later reissue added 'All Our Past Times' as well, along with non-essential recordings of two tedious onstage jams.

A full concert recorded in London in April 1977 was made available in 2012 on the 3 x CD 35th-anniversary deluxe reissue of *Slowhand*. This is very good indeed. That same month Eric and his band performed an hour-long live set for the venerable BBC TV show *The Old Grey Whistle Test*. Eric looks restless despite (or perhaps because of) being seemingly well lubricated by Remy Martin. This can be easily found on YouTube and is one of the few visual records of Eric in concert in this period. Percussionist Sergio Pastora was a member of the band at this time.

A chaotic live session for Alexis Korner's fiftieth birthday party, 19 April 1978, was partially released as *The Party Album* in 1980. Eric plays on 'Hey, Pretty Mama', 'High Heel Sneakers' and 'Stormy Monday'.

1979's *Just One Night* is one of the great live albums of the 1970s. The presence of Albert Lee on second guitar and vocals, and pianist Chris Stainton, spur Clapton to play hard and loud. Most of the tracks are from Clapton's most recent studio albums, *Slowhand* and *Backless*, with added injections of powerful blues songs by Big Maceo Merriweather and Otis Rush. Worth revisiting.

In September 1981, Clapton recorded 'Crossroads', 'Cause We've Ended Up As Lovers' and 'Further On Up The Road' with Jeff Beck during *The Secret Policeman's Other Ball* benefit shows in London. The album *The Secret Policeman's Other Ball: The Music* documents this rare collaboration, along with another ensemble, 'I Shall Be Released'.

Time Pieces Vol. II: Live in the Seventies (1983) is a cash-in follow-up to RSO's successful *Time Pieces* 'best-of'. There's a tight version of 'Knockin' on Heaven's Door' from the *Just One Night* concert recording and the first release of Eric Clapton singing Charlie Chaplin's 'Smile' in 1974. Eric was one of many guests at Chuck Berry's 60th birthday concert in St. Louis on 16 October 1986. The album *Hail! Hail! Rock 'N' Roll* includes 'Wee Wee Hours' and 'Rock and Roll Music'. The film version adds 'Hail! Hail! Rock 'N' Roll'. The following month Eric guested with the Robert Cray Band at the Mean Fiddler in London. Their performance of Cray's 'Phone Booth' was given away as a flexi-disc with the May 1987 edition of *Guitar Player* magazine.

During his eighties renaissance, Clapton joined the 'house band' for several Prince's Trust Rock Galas. Albums of the 1986 and 1987 shows document Clapton performing with many, varied artists as well-performing two of his current songs: 'Tearing Us Apart' and 'Behind the Mask'. Eric also performed the first of these at a Tina Turner concert in June 1987, released on *Tina Live in Europe* the following year. His guest appearance at a Rolling Stones concert in Atlantic City, 19 December 1989, would be released on the live album *Flashpoint* (1990). This scintillating version of 'Little Red Rooster' rolls back the years. Clapton was one of many performers at the Silver Clef Award Winners Concert at Knebworth Park on 30 June 1990. His short set comprised 'Before You Accuse Me' and 'Tearing Us Apart'. He also plays on three songs by Dire Straits and two by Elton John.

24 Nights (1991) is a rather antiseptic document of the series of shows at the Royal Albert Hall in 1990 and 1991. Producer Russ Titelman splits the album into four sections, each with different bands, so you never really get any continuity or more than 22 minutes of each line-up. Junior Wells' 'Hoodoo Man' and Buddy Guy's 'Watch Yourself' are rare performances from the blues set, but perhaps of more interest are the three tracks recorded with the National Philharmonic Orchestra on 9 February 1990. That entire concert was broadcast on BBC Radio One. This is still the only place to hear Michael Kamen's marvellous 'Concerto for Electric Guitar and Orchestra'.

Clapton and his band backed up George Harrison during a series of twelve live dates in Japan in December 1991. The album *Live in Japan* shows both Eric and George in fine form.

Unplugged (1992), recorded 16 January 1992, garnered some of the best reviews of Clapton's career. Greg Kot of the Chicago Tribune is perhaps harsh when he called *Unplugged* a 'blues album for Yuppies'. Clapton is relaxed, his band is fantastic, and the song selections and performances are superlative. 'Tears in Heaven' here is a career highlight: Clapton's singing is flawless. *Unplugged* won three Grammy awards at the 35th Annual Grammy Awards in 1993 and became the bestselling live album of all time, selling 26 million copies worldwide. An expanded edition, released in 2013, adds six further performances, including previously unheard versions of 'Circus', 'My Father's Eyes' and 'Worried Life Blues'. Clapton accepted his Grammys mid-way through an annual residency at the Royal Albert Hall. Two songs from this series of concerts–'32-20 Blues' and 'County Jail'–were released in late 1994 on the CD single 'Motherless Child'.

Clapton was one of many very famous contributors to Bobfest, officially The 30th Anniversary Concert Celebration, a star-laden concert commemorating the music of Bob Dylan held at Madison Square Garden on 16 October 1992. Clapton played scintillating and effortlessly melodic versions of 'Don't Think Twice, It's All Right' and 'Love Minus Zero/No Limit', as well as performing on 'My Back Pages' with the alarming sextuplet-threat line-up of Bob Dylan, Roger McGuinn, Tom Petty, Neil Young, Eric Clapton and George Harrison. The live album includes the first and last of these. The 2014 reissue adds a rehearsal take of 'Don't Think Twice, It's All Right' where the sparks really fly.

1995's live concert tribute to Stevie Ray Vaughan, recorded in Austin, Texas would be released in 1996. Clapton performs Vaughan's 'Ain't Gone 'N' Give

Up on Your Love' and joins in with Robert Cray, Dr John, Buddy Guy, B. B. King, Art Neville, Bonnie Raitt and Jimmie Vaughan for 'Six Strings Down', 'Tick Tock' and 'SRV Shuffle'. The last named won Best Rock Instrumental Performance at the 39th Annual Grammy Awards. *Crossroads 2: Live in the Seventies* (1996) collects thirty-one unreleased live performances from 1974, 1975, 1977 and 1978 across four CDs, including the first-ever release of 'Loving You Has Made My Life Sweeter Than Ever', and a jam with Carlos Santana. Four studio outtakes add to the collectability of this box set.

The album *Pavarotti and Friends for War Child* pairs Eric with Luciano Pavarotti and the East London Choir for 'Holy Mother', and with Sheryl Crow on her song 'Run Baby Run'. These were recorded in Modena in 1996. *Live in Hyde Park* is a 1997 video-only release of a concert from the previous summer.

Clapton and Crow would appear together again in 1998 and 1999. *A Very Special Christmas Live* was recorded live at a benefit event in Washington, DC, in December 1998. Clapton adds guitar to a bluesy 'Merry Christmas Baby'. Eric also plays on a version of Canned Heat's 'Christmas Blues' with Blues Traveler's Jon Popper, sings a stately 'Christmas Tears' himself, and joins Tracey Chapman for an excellent duet of 'Give Me One Reason'. There's also the inevitable all-star finale: Eric sings a few lines of 'Santa Claus Is Coming to Town' and spits a few guitar licks. Clapton appeared with Crow at a concert in New York's Central Park in September 1999. *Sheryl Crow and Friends: Live from Central Park* includes 'White Room' and a shambolic all-hands-on-deck version of 'Tombstone Blues'.

One More Car, One More Rider (2002) documents the 2001 world tour, with a set split three ways: six acoustic songs including versions of 'Tears in Heaven' and 'Change the World', five new(ish) electric tracks, and seven classics, finishing with a delicate and sincere reading of 'Over the Rainbow'. Clapton's singing is brilliant throughout. A DVD is available of this and all subsequent live albums.

The Concert for New York City at Madison Square Garden on 20 October 2001 brought together many famous musicians. Eric appeared with Buddy Guy to perform 'Hoochie Coochie Man' and is featured on 'Freedom' by Paul McCartney. Both were released on CD and DVD. Eric performs on three songs on *Party at the Palace* (2002).

The *Concert for George* on 29 November 2002 was an emotionally charged and musically rich tribute to Clapton's ex-husband-in-law George Harrison who had died the year before. Clapton sings and plays peerlessly: his contribution to Anoushka Shankar's 'Arpan' is astounding, and the versions of 'Isn't It a Pity' and 'While My Guitar Gently Weeps' are quite, quite wonderful.

Eric guested with Zucchero at the Royal Albert Hall in 2003, repeating his guest appearance on 'Wonderful World' and spraying blues guitar all over a strong 'Hey Man'. These are on the DVD *Zu & Co. Live at The Royal Albert Hall* (2004). Eric sings a duet with Willie Nelson on 'Night Life' from Nelson's *Live and Kickin'* album, recorded in April 2003.

Perhaps increasingly aware of the mortality of his peers, Clapton spent several years paying tribute to his influences and peers (or making albums with them).

Rolling Stone: Do you feel you are looking back because you can see more clearly?
Eric: I think that is true. My sobriety now is getting to be longer than my drinking period. I almost forget that the way I think and act now is different – a hundred per cent different. So yeah, there was a lot of unfinished business that needs to be resolved, cleared up, made amends for. But it is a result of the changed way that I think now.

In this vein Clapton participated in a series of concerts with his key early collaborators between 2000 and 2011. Almost thirty years after the end of Derek and the Dominos, Clapton reunited with Bobby Whitlock for three songs on *Later With Jools Holland* in April 2000, including a definitive 'Bell Bottom Blues'. Three years later Clapton performed eight songs in concert with John Mayall available on the *70th Birthday Concert* DVD. It had been almost forty years since Clapton had last performed live with Mayall. And in 2005, Clapton surprised many with reunion concerts with Cream thirty-six years after their initial break-up. This gave us the almost overwhelmingly brilliant *Royal Albert Hall London May 2-3-5-6, 2005,* which has all of the fire of the 1960s, but now with oodles of craft and commitment and none of the showboating. Eric is pushed hard by a rejuvenated world-class rhythm section. *Live from Madison Square Garden* (2009) is a thrilling album recording on Clapton's 2008 tour with Steve Winwood, the first full Winwood-Clapton concerts in almost forty years. Want to hear Clapton cut loose on 'Voodoo Chile'? Here it is, along with tracks from Blind Faith, Traffic, Derek and the Dominos, their solo careers and, best of all, a scintillating cover of Buddy Miles' 'Them Changes'. They played further dates together in 2009, 2010 and 2011.

Later in 2008 Eric joined Jeff Back at Ronnie Scott's in London to play some warm, sizzling blues on 'Little Brown Bird' and 'You Need Love'. These can be heard and/or seen on the *Performing This Week* CD and DVD. They would perform some joint concerts in London, New York, Toronto and Montreal in 2010. A version of 'Further On Up the Road' with Joe Bonamassa appears on the 2009 video *Joe Bonamassa: Live From The Royal Albert Hall*. Worth tracking down if you're feeling flush, is the forty-seven CD *Beacon Box* of fifteen shows by the Allman Brothers Band, recorded at the Beacon Theatre in New York in March 2009. Eric Clapton guests at two of these shows: on 19 March he performed 'Key to the Highway', 'Dreams', 'Why Does Love Got To Be So Sad', 'Little Wing', Any Day' and 'Layla'. The following night it was 'Key To The Highway', 'Stormy Monday', 'Dreams', 'Why Does Love Got To Be So Sad', 'Little Wing', In Memory of Elizabeth Reed', and 'Layla'. These are phenomenally good. *Play the Blues: Live from Jazz at Lincoln Center*

(2011) pairs Clapton with Wynton Marsalis at a concert in September 2011. The combination of British blues and American jazz works well, although the version of 'Layla' here transforms that classic song into a dirge. 2014's *Plane, Trains and Eric* is a DVD-only release which provides a mixture of interviews, backstage footage and live concert performances by Clapton and his band as they travel through the Far East and Middle East.

Slowhand at 70 – Live at The Royal Albert Hall (2015) offers a slickly performed document of an entertaining but inessential show of a man finally starting to look and feel his age. A concert from March 2007 would be released ten years after the fact as *Live in San Diego* (2017). This presents a full show from the tremendous Derek & Doyle Tour, including six songs from *Layla and Other Assorted Love Songs* and guest appearances from J. J. Cale and Robert Cray.

A three-CD box set released in 2016 presents highlights of the Crossroads festivals of 2004 (Dallas), 2007 (Chicago), 2010 (Chicago) and 2013 (New York City). Clapton appears on almost half of these, either as a solo performer or with his guests, who include Jeff Beck, J. J. Cale, Gary Clark Jr, Robert Cray, Billy Gibbons, Vince Gill, Buddy Guy, B. B. King, John Mayer, Carlos Santana, Joe Walsh, Ronnie Wood and Jimmie Vaughan. This is complimented by a second three-CD set from 2020, which documents the 2019 festival at American Airlines Center in Dallas. Clapton plays some old favourites, including acoustic versions of 'Wonderful Tonight' and 'Lay Down Sally' with Andy Fairweather Low. He also paid tribute to George Harrison, joining Peter Frampton for 'While My Guitar Gently Weeps', and to Prince in a brilliant rendition of 'Purple Rain'.

Compilations

Eric Clapton's music has been anthologised many times by his three principal record companies: Decca (1965-1966), RSO (1966-1982), and Duck/Reprise (1982-2013).

The History of Eric Clapton (1972) is a double album, carefully compiled with tracks by The Yardbirds, John Mayall's Bluesbreakers, Cream, Blind Faith, Delaney and Bonnie, and Derek and the Dominos. There are unreleased or hard-to-find tracks such as 'I Want to Know' by The Powerhouse, 'Teasin'' by King Curtis, the Phil Spector version of 'Tell the Truth' and an unreleased jam version of the same song: this was the only place to find this version for eighteen years. *Eric Clapton at His Best* (1972) is a US-only double album compiling tracks from just three albums: *Blind Faith*, *Eric Clapton*, and *Layla and Other Assorted Love Songs*. The following year's *Clapton*, long out of print, reshuffles eight of the same tracks.

The Blues World of Eric Clapton (1975) and *Steppin' Out* (1981) both collect material recorded for Decca with John Mayall's Bluesbreakers, along with sessions for Otis Spann and Champion Jack Dupree.

Timepieces: The Best of Eric Clapton (1982) is a solo singles greatest hits collection – it collects eleven singles released between 1970 and 1978, including the first album release of 'Knockin' on Heaven's Door'. Two years later, *Backtrackin'* (1984) covers the same ground but adds some classics by Cream and Derek and the Dominos, as well as a handful of live tracks.

The Cream of Eric Clapton (1987) is a hugely successful 17-track compilation, the first Clapton compilation to be released on CD after his mid-80s renaissance. It includes his recent top twenty hit 'Behind the Mask' and sold over a million copies in the UK. This was followed a few months later by the immense career retrospective box set *Crossroads* (1988). With seventy-three tracks across four CDs, the set includes his work with the Yardbirds, John Mayall and the Bluesbreakers, Cream, Blind Faith, Delaney and Bonnie and Friends, and Derek and the Dominos, as well as his solo career. There were many unreleased or uncollected tracks, including five from the unfinished second Derek and the Dominos album. RSO followed this up with a second box set in 1996 called *Crossroads 2: Live in the Seventies*, which includes over thirty unreleased live tracks recorded between 1974 and 1978, and four previously unreleased studio tracks from the same period.

Story (1991) and *The Cream of Clapton* (1995) reshuffle the RSO material once again. The much more interesting *Blues* (1999), pairs previously released studio tracks and live performances with five unheard studio tracks.

Clapton Chronicles: The Best of Eric Clapton (1999) collects sixteen songs from 1985 to 1999 and includes two new tracks. This reached number six in his home country. An updated two-disc version from 2006 selects another thirteen tracks, but with no surprises. *Complete Clapton* (2007) has a disc of RSO material from 1966 to 1981–all familiar from many previous compilations–and a disc of Reprise tracks from 1983 to 2006, which mostly repeats *Clapton*

Chronicles. Forever Man (2015) expands *Clapton Chronicles* to three discs with over fifty tracks through to 2012, including a superb selection of post-1983 blues recordings. There are only a handful of overlaps with 1988's *Crossroads*, so for a comprehensive fifty-year career overview, then *Crossroads* and *Forever Man* are the places to start.

Finally, *Life in 12 Bars* is a double CD set that accompanies Lili Fini Zanuck's illuminating 2017 documentary about Clapton's life and music. Familiar tracks by Clapton's pre-solo bands are joined by some of his early influences (Big Bill Broonzy, Muddy Waters), session work for others (Aretha Franklin, The Beatles, George Harrison), and just four post-1974 solo tracks. These include the otherwise unreleased full-length 'I Shot the Sheriff', and a first-time release of a ragged, drunkenly embarrassing take on Chuck Berry's 'Little Queenie', recorded in Long Beach in July 1974.

Epilogue

Eric Clapton's career in music has lasted almost sixty years. He is the only three-time inductee to the Rock and Roll Hall of Fame, credited to his work with the Yardbirds, Cream, and as a solo artist. Of his early-sixties rock music contemporaries, perhaps only Paul McCartney and the Rolling Stones can claim to have enjoyed the same continuous commercial success.

Many of his friends and peers are gone. George Harrison (2001), Tom Dowd (2002), Jim Capaldi (2005), Billy Preston (2006), J. J. Cale (2013), Jack Bruce (2014), B. B. King (2015), Leon Russell (2016), Prince (2016), Don Williams (2017), Gregg Allman (2017), Tom Petty (2017), Ginger Baker (2019), Peter Green (2020), Jamie Oldaker (2020). At the time of writing his mentors Buddy Guy and John Mayall are 86 and 87.

His marriage to Melia McEnery in January 2002 finally gave Clapton the family life he had craved for so long. He is now the father to four daughters, three with Melia. His public activity, quite naturally, has declined. Who could blame Eric Clapton for wanting a quiet retirement with his young family? As he told *Loudersound.com* in 2016:

It's been a good ride. And I'm still here. At the moment, it's going along fine. My life is really blessed. I've got a wonderful family, a fantastically beautiful wife, in every way, great kids, and I can still play. I mean, it's hard work sometimes, the physical side of it – just getting old, man, is hard. But I love to play, still. I sit in the corner of our front room with a guitar, and I play in the morning and I rest in the afternoon ... Life is good.

Some Eric Clapton Playlists

Eric Plays J. J. Cale
'Somebody Knockin'' – from *I Still Do* (2016)
'After Midnight' – from *Crossroads* (1988)
'I'll Make Love to You Anytime' – from *Backless* (1978)
'Ride the River' – from *The Road to Escondido* (2006)
'Travelin' Light' – from *Pilgrim* (1998)
'Angel' – from *Old Sock* (2013)
'Missing Person' – from *The Road to Escondido* (2006)
'Dead End Road' – from *The Road to Escondido* (2006)
'Who Am I Telling You?' – from *Live in San Diego* (2016)
'Don't Cry Sister' – from *The Road to Escondido* (2006)
'Since You Said Goodbye' – from *The Breeze* (2014)
'Cocaine' – from *Just One Night* (1980)

Eric Plays Robert Johnson
'When You Got a Good Friend' – from *Me and Mr Johnson* (2004)
'Stop Breakin' Down Blues' – from *Sessions for Robert J* (2004)
'Stones in My Passway' – from *I Still Do* (2016)
'Me and the Devil Blues' – from *Sessions for Robert J* (2004)
'Steady Rollin' Man' – from *461 Ocean Boulevard* (1974)
'Walkin' Blues' – from *Unplugged* (1992)
'Ramblin' on My Mind' – from *Just One Night* (1980)
'Kind Hearted Woman Blues' – from *Sessions for Robert J* (2004)
'Love in Vain' – from *Sessions for Robert J* (2004)
'Hell Hound on My Trail' – from *Sessions for Robert J* (2004)
'Little Queen of Spades' – from *Live in San Diego* (2016)
'Malted Milk' – from *Unplugged* (1992)
'Crossroads' – from *Royal Albert Hall London May 2-3-5-6, 2005* (2005) by Cream

Eric Plays Dobro
'How Long Blues' – from *From the Cradle* (1994)
'Give Me Strength' – from *461 Ocean Boulevard* (1974)
'We've Been Told (Jesus Coming Soon)' – from *There's One in Every Crowd* (1975)
'Ramblin On My Mind' – from *Sessions for Robert J* (2004)
'They're Red Hot' – from *Me and Mr Johnson* (2004)
'Born to Lose' – from *Old Sock* (2016)
'One Track Mind' – from *Back Home* (2005)
'Pretty Girl' – from *Money and Cigarettes* (1983)
'Born in Time' – from *Pilgrim* (1998)
'Sign Language' – from *No Reason to Cry* (1976)
'Come On In My Kitchen' – from *Me and Mr Johnson* (2004)

'Please Me With Me' – from *461 Ocean Boulevard* (1974)
'Mean Old Frisco' – from *Slowhand* (1977)
'Hold Me Lord' – from *Another Ticket* (1981)
'Running on Faith' – from *Unplugged* (1992)
'Ruby' – from *Homeboy* (1988)

Eric Sings Standards
'Our Love Is Here to Stay' – from *Old Sock* (2013)
'When Somebody Thinks You're Wonderful' – from *Clapton* (2010)
'How Deep Is the Ocean' – from *Clapton* (2010)
'Rocking Chair' – from *Clapton* (2010)
'I Want a Little Girl' – from *Reptile* (2001)
'I'll Be Alright' – from *I Still Do* (2016)
'Just Walkin' in The Rain' – from *Good Rockin' Tonight: The Legacy of Sun Records* (2001)
'My Very Good Friend the Milkman' – from *Clapton* (2010)
'The Folks Who Live on the Hill' – from *Old Sock* (2013)
'All of Me' – from *Old Sock* (2013)
'Little Man, You've Had a Busy Day' – from *I Still Do* (2016)
'Autumn Leaves' – from *Clapton* (2010)
'I'll Be Seeing You' – from *I Still Do* (2016)
'Over the Rainbow' – from *One More Car, One More Rider* (2001)

Eric Plays Soul
'Inside of Me' – from *Pilgrim* (1998)
'Ain't Gonna Stand for It' – from *Reptile* (2001)
'What Would I Do Without You?' – from *Small World Big Band* (2001)
'Losing Hand' – from CD single of 'Ain't Gonna Stand for It' (2001)
'Piece of My Heart' – from *Back Home* (2005)
'I'm Going Left' – from *Back Home* (2005)
'You Must Believe Me' – from *A Tribute to Curtis Mayfield* (1994)
'River of Tears' – from *One More Car, One More Rider* (2001)
'Border Song' – from *Two Rooms: Celebrating the Songs of Elton John and Bernie Taupin* (1991)
'Needs His Woman' – from *Pilgrim* (1998)
'Don't Love Nobody' – from *Back Home* (2005)
'Broken Down' – from *Reptile* (2001)
'Lead Me On' – from *Journeyman* (1989)
'Don't Let Me Be Lonely Tonight' – from *Reptile* (2001)

Eric Plays Reggae
'I Shot the Sheriff' – from *Life in 12 Bars* (2017)
'Swing Low, Sweet Chariot' – from *There's One in Every Crowd* (1975)
'Whatcha Gonna Do' – from *Crossroads* (1988)

'Burial' from *Give Me Strength – The '74–'75 Recordings* (2013)
"Knocking on Heaven's Door' – from any one of loads of 'best of' albums
'Say What You Will' – from *Back Home* (2005)
'Revolution' – from *Back Home* (2005)
'Silver Rain' – from *Silver Rain* by Marcus Miller (2005)
'Further On Down the Road' – from *Old Sock* (2013)
'Till Your Well Runs Dry' – from *Old Sock* (2013)
'Your One and Only Man' – from *Old Sock* (2013)
'No Sympathy' – from *Old Sock* (deluxe edition) (2013)
'I Will Be There' – from *I Still Do* (2016)

Eric Plays Guitar
'Edge of Darkness' – from *Edge of Darkness* (1985)
'Just Like A Prisoner' – from *Behind the Sun* (1985)
'Five Long Years' – from *From the Cradle* (1994)
'Groaning the Blues' – from *From the Cradle* (1994)
'Someday After a While (You'll Be Sorry)' – from *From the Cradle* (1994)
'Sporting Life Blues' – from *The Road to Escondido* (2006)
'Ten Long Years' – from *Riding With the King* (2000)
'Can't Hold Out Much Longer' – from *Clapton* (2010)
'Still Got the Blues' – from *Old Sock* (2013)
'One Day' – from *Back Home* (2005)
'The Shape You're In' – from *Money & Cigarettes* (1983)
'Little Wing'– from *Beacon Box Set* (2009) with The Allman Brother Band
'Stone Free'– from *Stone Free: A Tribute to Jimi Hendrix* (1993)
'Burning of The Midnight Lamp' from *Power of Soul: A Tribute to Jimi Hendrix* (2004)
'Voodoo Chile'– from *Live From Madison Square Garden February 2008* (2008) with Steve Winwood
'We're Going Wrong' from *Royal Albert Hall, 2-3-5-6 2005* (2005) with Cream
'Diamonds Made from Rain' – from *Clapton* (2010)

Bibliography

Bowling, D., *Eric Clapton FAQ* (Backbeat Books, Milwaukee, 2013)

Boyd, P. with Junor, P., *Wonderful Tonight: George Harrison, Eric Clapton and Me* (Three Rivers Press, New York, 2008)

Clapton, E., *Eric Clapton: The Autobiography* (Broadway, New York, 2007)

Coleman, R., *Survivor–The Authorized biography of Eric Clapton* (Futura Publications, London, 1986)

Collins, P., *Not Dead Yet: The Autobiography* (Century St. Albans, 2016)

Christgau, R., *Christgau's Guide: Rock Albums of the Seventies* (Vermilion, London, 1982)

Conforth, B. and Wardlow, G., *Up Jumped the Devil: The Real Life of Robert Johnson* (Chicago Review Press, Chicago, 2019)

Frame, P. *Rock Family Trees* (Omnibus Press, London, 1980)

Hepworth, D., *Uncommon People: The Rise and Fall of the Rock Stars 1955-1994* (Black Swan, London, 2018)

Johns, G., *Sound Man* (Blue Rider Press, New York, 2014)

Madinger, C., and Easter, M., *Eight Arms to Hold You: The Solo Beatles Compendium* (44 1 Productions Inc, Chesterfield MO, 2001)

Norman P., *Slowhand: The Life and Music of Eric Clapton* (W&N, London, 2018)

Paul, A., *One Way Out–The Inside Story of the Allman Brothers Band* (St Martin's Griffin, London, 2015)

Radcliffe, R., *Crossroads: In Search of the Moments that Changed Music* (Canongate, London, 2020)

Roberty, M., *Eric Clapton-The New Visual Documentary* (Omnibus Press, London, 1990)

In his own words–Eric Clapton (Omnibus Press, London, 1993)

Eric Clapton-The Complete Recording Sessions 1963-1992 (Blandford, London, 1993)

The Eric Clapton Scrapbook (Citadel Press, New York, 1994)

Eric Clapton–The Complete Guide to His Music (Omnibus Press, London, 2005)

Shapiro, H., *Eric Clapton–Lost in the Blues* (Da Capo, Boston, 1992)

Wald, E., *Escaping the Delta: Robert Johnson and the Invention of the Blues* (Amistad, New York, 2005)

Whitlock, B. with Roberty, M., *A Rock 'n' Roll Autobiography* (McFarland & Co., Jefferson, 2010)

On Track series

Tori Amos – Lisa Torem 978-1-78952-142-9
Asia – Peter Braidis 978-1-78952-099-6
Barclay James Harvest – Keith and Monica Domone 978-1-78952-067-5
The Beatles – Andrew Wild 978-1-78952-009-5
The Beatles Solo 1969-1980 – Andrew Wild 978-1-78952-030-9
Blue Oyster Cult – Jacob Holm-Lupo 978-1-78952-007-1
Marc Bolan and T.Rex – Peter Gallagher 978-1-78952-124-5
Kate Bush – Bill Thomas 978-1-78952-097-2
Camel – Hamish Kuzminski 978-1-78952-040-8
Caravan – Andy Boot 978-1-78952-127-6
Eric Clapton Solo – Andrew Wild 978-1-78952-141-2
The Clash – Nick Assirati 978-1-78952-077-4
Crosby, Stills and Nash – Andrew Wild 978-1-78952-039-2
The Damned – Morgan Brown 978-1-78952-136-8
Deep Purple and Rainbow 1968-79 – Steve Pilkington 978-1-78952-002-6
Dire Straits – Andrew Wild 978-1-78952-044-6
The Doors – Tony Thompson 978-1-78952-137-5
Dream Theater – Jordan Blum 978-1-78952-050-7
Elvis Costello and The Attractions – Georg Purvis 978-1-78952-129-0
Emerson Lake and Palmer – Mike Goode 978-1-78952-000-2
Fairport Convention – Kevan Furbank 978-1-78952-051-4
Peter Gabriel – Graeme Scarfe 978-1-78952-138-2
Genesis – Stuart MacFarlane 978-1-78952-005-7
Gentle Giant – Gary Steel 978-1-78952-058-3
Gong – Kevan Furbank 978-1-78952-082-8
Hawkwind – Duncan Harris 978-1-78952-052-1
Roy Harper – Opher Goodwin 978-1-78952-130-6
Iron Maiden – Steve Pilkington 978-1-78952-061-3
Jethro Tull – Jordan Blum 978-1-78952-016-3
Elton John in the 1970s – Peter Kearns 978-1-78952-034-7
Gong – Kevan Furbank 978-1-78952-082-8
The Incredible String Band – Tim Moon 978-1-78952-107-8
Iron Maiden – Steve Pilkington 978-1-78952-061-3
Judas Priest – John Tucker 978-1-78952-018-7
Kansas – Kevin Cummings 978-1-78952-057-6
Level 42 – Matt Philips 978-1-78952-102-3
Aimee Mann – Jez Rowden 978-1-78952-036-1
Joni Mitchell – Peter Kearns 978-1-78952-081-1
The Moody Blues – Geoffrey Feakes 978-1-78952-042-2
Mike Oldfield – Ryan Yard 978-1-78952-060-6
Tom Petty – Richard James 978-1-78952-128-3
Queen – Andrew Wild 978-1-78952-003-3
Renaissance – David Detmer 978-1-78952-062-0
The Rolling Stones 1963-80 – Steve Pilkington 978-1-78952-017-0
Steely Dan – Jez Rowden 978-1-78952-043-9
Steve Hackett – Geoffrey Feakes 978-1-78952-098-9
Thin Lizzy – Graeme Stroud 978-1-78952-064-4
Toto – Jacob Holm-Lupo 978-1-78952-019-4

Also available from Sonicbond

U2 – Eoghan Lyng 978-1-78952-078-1
UFO – Richard James 978-1-78952-073-6
The Who – Geoffrey Feakes 978-1-78952-076-7
Roy Wood and the Move – James R Turner 978-1-78952-008-8
Van Der Graaf Generator – Dan Coffey 978-1-78952-031-6
Yes – Stephen Lambe 978-1-78952-001-9
Frank Zappa 1966 to 1979 – Eric Benac 978-1-78952-033-0
10CC – Peter Kearns 978-1-78952-054-5

Decades Series
Alice Cooper in the 1970s – Chris Sutton 978-1-78952-104-7
Curved Air in the 1970s – Laura Shenton 978-1-78952-069-9
Fleetwood Mac in the 1970s – Andrew Wild 978-1-78952-105-4
Focus in the 1970s – Stephen Lambe 978-1-78952-079-8
Marillion in the 1980s – Nathaniel Webb 978-1-78952-065-1
Pink Floyd In The 1970s – Georg Purvis 978-1-78952-072-9
The Sweet in the 1970s – Darren Johnson 978-1-78952-139-9
Uriah Heep in the 1970s – Steve Pilkington 978-1-78952-103-0

On Screen series
Carry On… – Stephen Lambe 978-1-78952-004-0
David Cronenberg – Patrick Chapman 978-1-78952-071-2
Doctor Who: The David Tennant Years – Jamie Hailstone 978-1-78952-066-8
Monty Python – Steve Pilkington 978-1-78952-047-7
Seinfeld Seasons 1 to 5 – Stephen Lambe 978-1-78952-012-5

Other Books
Babysitting A Band On The Rocks – G.D. Praetorius 978-1-78952-106-1
Derek Taylor: For Your Radioactive Children – Andrew Darlington 978-1-78952-038-5
Iggy and The Stooges On Stage 1967-1974 – Per Nilsen 978-1-78952-101-6
Jon Anderson and the Warriors – the road to Yes – David Watkinson 978-1-78952-059-0
Nu Metal: A Definitive Guide – Matt Karpe 978-1-78952-063-7
Tommy Bolin: In and Out of Deep Purple – Laura Shenton 978-1-78952-070-5
Maximum Darkness – Deke Leonard 978-1-78952-048-4
Maybe I Should've Stayed In Bed – Deke Leonard 978-1-78952-053-8
The Twang Dynasty – Deke Leonard 978-1-78952-049-1

and many more to come!

Would you like to write for Sonicbond Publishing?

We are mainly a music publisher, but we also occasionally publish in other genres including film and television. At Sonicbond Publishing we are always on the look-out for authors, particularly for our two main series, On Track and Decades.

Mixing fact with in depth analysis, the On Track series examines the entire recorded work of a particular musical artist or group. All genres are considered from easy listening and jazz to 60s soul to 90s pop, via rock and metal.

The Decades series singles out a particular decade in an artist or group's history and focuses on that decade in more detail than may be allowed in the On Track series.

While professional writing experience would, of course, be an advantage, the most important qualification is to have real enthusiasm and knowledge of your subject. First-time authors are welcomed, but the ability to write well in English is essential.

Sonicbond Publishing has distribution throughout Europe and North America, and all our books are also published in E-book form. Authors will be paid a royalty based on sales of their book. Further details about our books are available from www.sonicbondpublishing.com. To contact us, complete the contact form there or email info@sonicbondpublishing.co.uk